THE
INTERVIEWER'S
HANDBOOK

Dedication

For my husband, Neil, who is the most wonderful human being and without whose amazing strength, help and support this book would never have been written.

THE INTERVIEWER'S HANDBOOK

Successful interviewing techniques for the workplace

Sandra Bunting

**KOGAN
PAGE**

London and Sterling, VA

First published in Great Britain and the United States in 2005 by Kogan Page Limited

120 Pentonville Road
London N1 9JN
United Kingdom
www.kogan-page.co.uk

22883 Quicksilver Drive
Sterling VA 20166-2012
USA

ISBN 0 7494 4293 X

British Library Cataloguing-in-Publication Data

A CIP record for this book is available from the British Library.

Library of Congress Cataloging-in-Publication Data

Bunting, Sandra, 1947–
    The interviewer's handbook: successful techniques for every work situation/
Sandra Bunting.
        p.cm.
    Includes bibliographical references and index.
    ISBN 0-7494-4293-X
    1. Employment interviewing. 2. Interviewing. I. Title.
HF5549.5.I6B86 2005
658.3'1124 – dc22

2005001794

Typeset by Datamatics Technologies Ltd, Mumbai, India
Printed and bound in Great Britain by Creative Print and Design (Wales), Ebbw Vale

Contents

Part 1

Interview preparation

1

Questioning techniques

In order to elicit relevant and comprehensive information from individuals during any interview process, it is important to use appropriate questioning techniques.

Conversation can be stimulated by one person, who may be sharing specific facts with others, or be expressing their feelings or opinions. An individual can show their thoughts, or contrast them through making a number of statements and offering their views on a specific topic. In addition, asking or answering questions can stimulate conversation. During the course of natural conversation, the flow of information is generated by a variety of verbal mechanisms.

Interviews cannot be considered natural conversations. All interviews take place to assist in gathering relevant information from an interviewee. This could be in relation to recruitment of staff; appraisal of staff; accident investigation, or in a variety of other circumstances. Usually, interviews are designed to discover specific information, which is identified and stated in the interview objective(s). Using effective questioning techniques therefore, the interviewer must strive to make the exchange of information seem as natural as possible, whilst at the same time, steering the conversation through a predetermined structure.

Since the task is to stimulate and guide the conversation, it is necessary to rely on one of the most basic mechanisms for creating conversation – that of using questions.

By using questions skilfully and subtly, it will be possible to elicit the information required whilst allowing the interviewee(s) to remain at ease during the interview. Being able to sustain the ease of the interviewee(s) is extremely effective in removing the 'unnatural' aspect of interviews.

TYPES OF QUESTION

The interviewer can call on a range of question types in an attempt to stimulate and guide the conversation.

Closed questions

Closed questions will yield little information. If an interviewer is attempting to obtain a quantity of information (in accident investigation, for example), or tease out attitudes (in recruitment interviewing), this is the least appropriate technique to use.

Closed questions have a valid use when properly controlled. They provide an economical way of verifying what the other person has done, said, or thinks. They also provide the opportunity to clarify any specific points economically.

The number of possible answers that could be given in response to a closed question is often small and predictable. For example:

Q   'Did you think the last Works Committee Meeting was useful?'

The expected response can only be:

A   'Yes' (or 'No')

Open questions

Using an 'open' questioning technique increases the number of possible responses an interviewer can expect. It is then open to the interviewee to choose an appropriate response. This then gives the interviewer the opportunity to make judgements based on their response. In its most basic form, an open question would begin:

'Tell me about..,........................?'

The probability of getting a larger volume of information from an open question is much greater than that offered by a closed question.

The following example of an open question leaves the respondent with no opportunity to answer with a simple 'Yes' or 'No', but expects them to give more detailed information:

Q   'What did you think of the last Works Committee Meeting?'

A   'Well, a bit hard going, but I managed to clarify some of the issues that had been troubling me.'

Or:

A   'To be honest, a complete waste of time. If I hadn't had to be there, I could have started to clear the mountain of paperwork and e-mails that seem to drop onto my desk every day.'

A crude rule of thumb is – the more open questions you ask the greater the quantity and quality of information you are likely to get. Typically, an open question will begin with one of the following:

WHO
WHAT
WHEN
WHERE
WHY, or
HOW

Probing questions

Probing questions are used as a natural follow-up to open questions. Having stimulated the interviewee to talk, you may wish to pursue a particular point that was only touched upon during the interview.

The probe question causes the individual to focus on the point that interests you, and results in more information being given. In its most basic form, the probe question would begin in the same way as an open question:

'Tell me more about...........................?'

More advanced probing questions again would begin with **WHO, WHAT, WHEN, WHERE, WHY,** or **HOW.** For example:

Q   'What did you think of the last Works Committee meeting?'

A   'Well, a bit hard going, but I managed to clarify some of the issues that had been troubling me.'

Q   'I'm pleased that you found it useful. What were the issues that had been troubling you?'

Having started to question an interviewee on a particular topic, it is important not to take things at face value and simply accept their initial response as the whole story. Your assessment of the information gathered during the interview should be based on the sound evidence gathered. Follow-up questioning can give you more complete and reliable information. For example:

- Where an interviewee is a little reticent or lacking in confidence, or perhaps even undervalues their skills ('I just do the photo-copying and filing... '). Filing is an important aspect of their work if documents are to be located quickly and easily in the future.
- Where the interviewee is not being wholly truthful by omitting pertinent information ('There are 10 people in my section', but they may only supervise five of these).
- When an interviewee does have more to offer but has not been able to relate this to the particular question that was asked, and

has been given inadequate opportunity to highlight relevant skills, knowledge and experience that they possess.

An example of how the probe questioning technique might be used in a recruitment interview is explained and illustrated in Figure 1.1, using a 'funnel' approach. The questions are designed to elicit more and more detailed information from the interviewee. The funnel approach continues to tighten and pin down specific detail. In this instance, the criterion for which evidence is being sought is concerned with effective budget management.

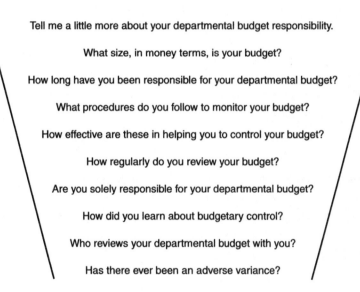

Tell me a little more about your departmental budget responsibility.

What size, in money terms, is your budget?

How long have you been responsible for your departmental budget?

What procedures do you follow to monitor your budget?

How effective are these in helping you to control your budget?

How regularly do you review your budget?

Are you solely responsible for your departmental budget?

How did you learn about budgetary control?

Who reviews your departmental budget with you?

Has there ever been an adverse variance?

Figure 1.1   Example of the probe questioning technique

Note: The probing technique is an aspect of interviewing that can often feel awkward. It is important that the interviewer practises this technique to become proficient in its use.

Leading questions

A leading question is one that expects the respondent to reply in a particular way. The wording of the question will indicate the required response. Examples of leading questions are:

Q   'Can I take it you've had no problems managing a budget?'
Q   'Meetings are a terrible waste of time, don't you think?'

Leading questions may result in answers that the interviewer would prefer to hear but are not necessarily representative of how the interviewee might respond to a question that was posed using the open questioning technique.

Multiple questions

Multiple questions tend to combine a number of questions in one. This can confuse an interviewee and also result in the individual forgetting one or more elements of the question. In addition, they may well not answer all aspects of the question fully. An example would be:

Q   'How do you think a supervisor's role fits in with a flatter organization structure and what are the pros and cons of introducing self-managing teams as opposed to line management?'

It is unlikely that an interviewee would manage to answer such a question fully or that the interviewer will elicit adequate useful information effectively using this approach.

Marathon questions

Marathon questions tend to be long-winded. They are usually questions that take you in a direction of no real value, and generally arise from lack of preparation. An example would be:

Q   'What is your opinion of appraisal schemes? I mean, do you think that they should be linked to pay or where do you see performance-related pay fitting in otherwise?'

Again, interviewees will find such questions difficult to follow and will be confused about how best to respond.

Trick questions

Some interviewers resort to using trick questions. 'Playing games' with interviewees, particularly during recruitment interviews, does not often assist in helping to identify the most appropriate candidate for a job. The purpose of all interviews is to gather as much relevant information as possible and to establish facts. Trick questions do nothing to assist in this quest and simply waste time. An example of a trick question would be:

Q 'What about meetings?'

A confident interviewee might actually respond with 'Well, what about meetings?' but that is unlikely and the net result is more likely to be one of confusion.

Multiple-choice questions

Multiple-choice questions give a number of alternative answers from which an individual is expected to choose. Multiple-choice questions are notoriously difficult to construct and should be used only in appropriate circumstances. Some examinations test knowledge using the multiple-choice approach. An example of a multiple-choice question used in a recruitment interview situation would be:

Q 'Are you interested in this post because of:

A Choose one from the following options:

1. the salary and benefits package offered;
2. as an opportunity to enhance your career;
3. to move into this field of operation'.

Of course, despite the three alternatives offered, none of these may be relevant to a particular candidate. There may be a different reason, but this approach gives the individual no opportunity to explain what that might be.

Task

Take the role of Personnel Manager in a small engineering company.

1. Develop five multiple-choice questions to test relevant knowledge of individuals who have applied for the post of Personal Assistant to you.
2. Test your questions on a willing volunteer or two to see whether they are constructed appropriately or whether there are queries regarding the meaning of the questions or the choice of answers available.

SUMMARIZING

During the interview process, whether the purpose is recruitment, accident investigation or for another purpose, it is important that the interviewer checks regularly to clarify with the interviewee the meaning of what has been said. This helps to clarify points that may have been misunderstood, but it is also very positive for the interviewee, who will be able to further explain any issues that they may have been unable to voice during the question and answer process.

INTERVENING

Intervening during the interview process is probably the most difficult of all to do effectively. An interviewee may ramble on because of nervousness or emotion and the interviewer loses the thread of what the interviewee was trying to convey. In addition, the interviewee may also lose their way in trying to get across one or more points.

Using non-verbal signals, such as dropping eye contact, or raising one hand (to indicate 'be careful'), or leaning forward, may make the interviewee break from speaking. The interviewer should watch for a pause and then gently retrieve focus.

NOTE-TAKING

The interviewer will need to develop strategies for organizing note-taking during the interview process. Notes provide a record of what has occurred during an interview.

In most interview situations it is inappropriate to concentrate on note-taking to the extent that you lose eye contact and the note-taking becomes an intrusion. Note-taking is an important aspect of any interview process, so it is important that the notes are not so brief that they are meaningless, both to you and to everyone else afterwards.

Two tips, which may prove useful for selection interviewing in particular, are:

■ When you are leading the questioning, arrange for one of the other interviewers to take responsibility for making notes, then change round.

■ Structure interview times so that there is adequate time for you to complete your notes before you move on to interview the next candidate.

Whatever strategies you adopt, the notes you take during an interview are a crucial aspect of the process. Therefore, it is important to develop strategies that are appropriate in each case.

Task

Millie Clarke is the office cleaner. She has had a minor accident on the premises having slipped and bruised her hip.

Generate a range of relevant questions that allow you to establish exactly what happened. Remember to use a range of questioning techniques to establish specific details and facts.

Scenario 1 – Javad Foods

In your role as Personnel Officer at Javad Foods, you are responsible for recruitment of all production personnel. You are interviewing a potential Assistant Supervisor/Team Leader and are trying to establish their level of experience in a similar environment. They will need to lead a team of 20 production operatives.

Scenario 2 – The Licensed Trade Recruitment Agency

You are a member of the team at The Licensed Trade Recruitment Agency and are interviewing potential Tenant Managers on behalf of one of your large Brewery clients. You need to establish their ability to manage a pub environment in a city centre location where Saturday nights can become a little 'rowdy'.

Scenario 3 – Green Lettuce Inc

You are responsible for recruitment at Green Lettuce Inc, and are interviewing potential candidates to fill a vacancy that requires the applicant to have experience and extensive knowledge of relevant horticultural environments.

Scenario 4 – The Leung Shoe Company Limited

You are responsible for recruitment and training at The Leung Shoe Company Limited and are interviewing potential candidates for the post of Manager for one of your company's larger units. Eight staff work at the branch and you need to establish the ability of candidates to manage both the people and the branch budget effectively.

Task

1. In each of the above four scenarios, generate appropriate probing questions, using the funnel technique explained and illustrated in Figure 1.1.
2. Where feasible, use the questions you have generated to practise your technique with other members of the personnel team within your own organization.

Case study: Fairview Electricals

Sally Friend is the Receptionist at Fairview Electricals. She has been employed by the company for five years and has proved to be a reliable and hard working individual. However, she has been absent from work for four days during the last month, and on closer investigation, you find that she was absent on the same day each week. This is not usual for Sally and you decide to find out what is causing these unauthorized absences from work.

Task

1. What initial steps do you propose to take in the Fairview Electricals case above?
2. Develop appropriate questions that will encourage Sally to openly discuss her unexplained absences.

2

Communication and listening techniques

EFFECTIVE COMMUNICATION

For any communication to be effective it has to be a two-way process. Deciding what information to communicate and also how that information will be imparted are crucial in ensuring that the message is received and interpreted correctly. Whether the information is communicated orally, in writing or via diagrams or pictures, it must be written clearly and in language that can be understood by all individuals who will see or hear it.

The way that the message is communicated will depend upon a number of factors, such as:

- the time available;
- the complexity of the information to be communicated;
- whether there is a need for the communication to be in writing or whether personal interaction is important;
- whether the information is confidential and/or how sensitive it is; and
- what the cost will be of getting the message to the intended audience.

If the communication is unclear it is likely that the individual(s) receiving it will misinterpret what is intended and subsequently, will also misinterpret what, if any, action is required. This will result in either incorrect action or no action being taken. There may be no response and in some instances, silence can indicate that incorrect interpretation has occurred, particularly if a response was expected.

In a conference situation, for example, where there may be a large amount of financial information to be communicated, the use of diagrams and charts will assist the audience to understand more effectively than any extensive verbal analysis of the detail.

Reasons why we communicate

We communicate for a variety of reasons, including:

- to initiate action by expressing what is required;
- to motivate and persuade others;
- to share information, ideas and beliefs in order to create awareness, understanding, and to persuade and influence others;
- to establish and maintain links with others and to foster and maintain trust, respect and cooperation, which lead to strong employee morale.

Individuals are more likely to listen and accept what is being said if the communication is credible and congenial. Credibility should be inherent within those individuals who are perceived as authority figures and who have a reputation, prestige, knowledge, expertise and experience in their given field of operation.

The ways that we communicate

Interpersonal communication can take place on a one-to-one basis, which is the most straightforward approach, particularly if this is face to face. However, a manager will also need to communicate effectively to members of his/her team and may also be required to communicate effectively with other groups, both within the organization and external to it. The team will also need to be able to communicate effectively with management. How this communication occurs will depend very much on the structure of the organization and how formal or informal the communication processes are.

Some successful organizations have found that talking to each other, rather than sending memos and e-mails, is a more effective way to communicate. This approach tends to be dynamic; decisions can be taken quickly and responses can be immediate. In these organizations, jobs get done that much more quickly.

Using documentation, whether that is paper or electronic, creates bureaucracy, which tends to slow down the decision-making process and creates delays in being able to respond to both internal and external queries and demands.

Mass communication, where the message is aimed at a large, diverse and geographically widespread audience can be delivered verbally, in writing or by using visuals. Whichever approach is adopted, care needs to be taken to ensure that the message conveyed is understood by all members of the intended audience, and therefore feedback is vital.

Problems in communicating effectively

Problems can occur in the communication cycle when the message becomes distorted. The message can become distorted by incorporating inappropriate language within the communication, such as technical terms, which might not be understood by all individuals. In addition, an audience can also misinterpret what is intended.

Distractions and interference can occur from chatter or conversations, breakdown of electronic equipment, and psychological noise. For instance, individuals can be distracted by thoughts that might be prejudicial, in addition to attitudes that may not be open to the message being communicated.

Factors that affect individuals, and that cause problems in communication are many. Some of these include:

- personality traits, which shape behaviour and attitudes;
- the level of education and training, which will be at varying levels for each individual;

- the role of an individual, where experience, knowledge and opportunity shapes their motivation;
- racial, ethnic and regional variations, which can create problems with language and understanding;
- socio-economic class, where there are differing values and levels of expectation.

This list is not definitive. There are many issues that could affect the communication process, which could ultimately lead to misunderstandings.

There are many other reasons why problems could occur, such as:

- the omission of pertinent information;
- including irrelevant information;
- non-verbal signals (gestures and body language) that detract from the intention of the communication;
- ineffective listening and reading skills;
- lack of credibility; and
- non-receipt of feedback.

All individuals within the organization who receive communications, whether they are verbal or written, can be selective in what they see and hear and can also misinterpret the message.

Barriers to effective communication

There are many factors that create barriers to effective communication. Some to consider include:

- Spans of control within the organization may be too wide and levels of authority might be unclear.
- Lines of communication may be too long and the message becomes distorted as it filters down through the layers. This is more often the case in larger organizations, particularly within bureaucratic organizations like the public sector for instance.
- The formal process of communication within the organization may be based on a formal organizational structure. This could prevent

those lower down the hierarchy being able to communicate directly with more senior personnel in other departments. This slows down decision-making and response times.

■ The organization's corporate objectives may be inconsistent, or these may not be expressed clearly and are therefore open to mis-interpretation.

Overcoming the barriers to effective communication

To improve communication, the organization structure may need to be simplified and/or strengthened and management will need to be open and clear in their communications. In addition, management must be persuaded and be seen to apply policies fairly across all levels of employee.

Lack of trust can create barriers through selective listening, distortion of the message, pre-supposition of the intended meaning of a communication and by manipulation. Fear creates mistrust.

Individuals might fear:

■ losing their status within the organization;
■ being misrepresented; or
■ showing gaps in their knowledge.

Barriers to effective communication can be overcome by:

■ ensuring that the management structure is organized effectively in line with the needs of the business;
■ ensuring that responsibility is well defined within the organization, and there are clear lines of communication;
■ ensuring that there is a willingness to consult, explain and consider individuals and their reactions in any communication;
■ ensuring that communications are specific and circulated in understandable language and in a form that is appropriate;
■ ensuring that the communication skills of the writer or speaker are strong and language skills are high.

Task

Review your organization structure:

1. Review your company's organization chart or create one that represents the current structure.
2. Are the spans of control clear and have these been communicated effectively to all staff?
3. Are the lines of communication clear and open? Is it easy for individuals to communicate effectively department to department?
4. Is the structure flat to facilitate speedy communications and decision-making? If not, what, in your opinion, can be done to create a more flexible, responsive organization, which can compete on speed as well as quality?
5. Consider what specific steps would need to be taken to improve communications within your organization.

Task

1. Identify the barriers to effective communication that exist within your own organization.
2. Can you identify strategies that you feel would overcome these barriers if they were adopted in the future?
3. How would you propose to develop and introduce the strategies you have identified to ensure that all employees within your organization clearly understand these and that there is no possibility of misinterpretation?

EFFECTIVE LISTENING

The assumption is that as we all have ears, we all listen. However, research has shown that an 'average' person remembers only 50 per cent of what they have heard.

There are three recognized approaches to effective listening:

1. *Attentive* listening relates primarily to paying close attention when receiving information.
2. *Active* listening where the aim is to appreciate the speaker's needs, feelings and emotions. This is particularly useful in any interview process.
3. *Critical* listening where the aim is to evaluate the strength of the message and its relevance.

If we are to listen effectively, we must:

■ fully concentrate on the key ideas and information that are being presented to us;
■ endeavour to remember the key words and concepts being communicated;
■ be able to keep an open mind and set aside bias to facilitate greater understanding of what is being said;
■ work hard to listen carefully:
   - resist distractions of any kind;
   - maintain eye contact with the speaker;
   - be responsive and react appropriately to what is being said;
   - observe the body language and other non-verbal signals displayed by the speaker; and
   - be willing to seek to confirm and clarify what has been said if the communication, or its meaning, is unclear.

Active listening

It is important to develop an *active* listening technique, especially during any interview process. We can improve our active listening ability if we decide that we will take part fully in all verbal communication interactions. Some of the advantages of developing effective listening skills include:

■ Adopting an active listening approach when relevant verbal communication is occurring will prove invaluable in circumstances

where we may need specific information for decision-making purposes in the future.

■ By communicating verbally, this speeds up the communication
process and gets things done much more quickly.

■ A person's tone of voice can help us to interpret the message(s)
being given.

■ It helps us to clarify any matters that are unclear – we can ask
questions and discuss issues.

■ The information received can be used to solve problems, create
new ideas and/or develop existing ones.

■ Verbal interaction helps us to build relationships and encourages
discussion as well as triggering spontaneity.

How can we listen?

Individuals tend to listen to conversation for a variety of reasons and
more especially if diverse views are sought on a particular issue
under discussion.

Effective listening skills are useful to make sure that the information being given is received, interpreted and used appropriately.
Listening skills help us to sort out information and identify information that is known to be incorrect.

Sometimes the way information is conveyed can distract us from
the underlying meaning of a message and it is important to listen for
a balanced argument to be put forward so that any documentary or
other evidence can be appraised effectively.

Task

Assessing your own listening approach.

1. How effectively do you listen to information that is being conveyed
   to you verbally?
2. How much of the information you have heard do you generally
   remember?
3. Do you often interrupt someone who is speaking?

Are you a born listener?

1. Do you pay close attention when others are talking?
2. When you sit next to someone you don't know at a meal do you always try to find an area of common interest to talk about?
3. Do you believe that everyone has something to share with you that has value for you – either now or in the future?
4. Can you set aside factors such as an individual's personality, tone of voice or the way they speak so that you are able to find out what he/she knows that may be of interest or use to you?
5. Are you a curious person – interested in people and ideas?
6. Do you respond with a smile, nod or word of encouragement as the speaker is talking to you?
7. Do you maintain good eye contact?
8. Do you take notes?
9. a) Do you understand your own prejudices, blind spots and assumptions?
   b) Are you aware that these can create problems for you as a listener?
   c) Do you control them?
10. Are you patient, particularly with people who have difficulty expressing themselves clearly?
11. 'The trouble with you is that you never listen.' How many times has this been said to you?

    – never
    – once
    – occasionally
    – often

12. Do you have an open mind in relation to other people's viewpoints?
13. Do you listen for emotional emphasis when someone is speaking as well as listening to the content?
14. Do you often reflect, re-state or paraphrase what a speaker has said to make sure that you have understood their meaning correctly?

All the above are indications of someone who is an *active* listener.

Task

1. How many of the approaches in the box on the previous page were you able to say honestly that you adopt?
2. What, if anything, do you need to do to improve your active listening technique for the future?

Task

What strategies will you adopt to listen more effectively during any interviews that you may conduct in the future?

Scenario – effective communication

Company handbooks (including staff handbooks) and manuals that contain either information about a process, or instructions about how to use specific equipment/carry out certain tasks, must be written clearly and succinctly to ensure that only relevant but comprehensive information/instructions are included.

Any company handbook or manual should:

- be clearly written using easy to understand language;
- include content that is relevant;
- ensure that information can be easily found;
- be affordable;
- be easy to revise and update as regularly as is necessary.

Task

1. Review any one of your company's existing handbooks or manuals. Do they conform to the above criteria?
2. If not, what needs to be done to revise this to ensure that it is clear and appropriate?

Case study: Opaque Polymers Limited

Opaque Polymers Limited produces paint, mainly for industrial use. Its customer base is mostly manufacturing industry and at the moment it is trying to meet a very large order from one of its five main customers.

Jim Carroll is the Production Manager and has just been informed by Larry Lane, one of his Supervisors, that a leak has occurred on one of the company's main paint lines and that the line has had to be stopped to facilitate repairs being carried out by members of the company's maintenance team.

Larry follows Jim Carroll to his office.

'Look Jim, I've got to be away shortly. It's my study day but someone needs to keep an eye on the maintenance guys, otherwise the line could be down all day.'

'When's Phil Potts due in?' Carroll asks.

'Not until this evening. He's on the nightshift this week, filling in for Paresh who's off sick.'

'I'd forgotten about Paresh,' Carroll says 'but look, we can't leave the line unmanned and I've just been called to a meeting with the Production Director. I've got to go – I'll see you later.'

Shortly after this exchange, Larry Lane leaves the premises.

When Jim Carroll gets back to the department some two hours later, Larry Lane has left, the line is still down and the maintenance team is on lunch.

Task

1. Analyse the breakdown in communication that has occurred in the Opaque Polymers case study above.
2. Suggest how communications could have been improved to ensure that there was adequate supervision of the line and that maintenance personnel remained on site until the line was up and running again.

Case study: Phillips Accountancy

Phillips Accountancy operates on a national basis from an office in a small rural town. Phillips counts among its clients, a famous chef, a top restaurant and a large recruitment agency in the capital city.

The company is family owned and consists of five main partners and 20 accounting personnel. Each partner has specific responsibilities and has access to all 20 accounting personnel. In addition, there are six trainee accountants who are at varying stages of development. There are five administrators and three personal assistants who, between them, deal with all paperwork generated by the partners and accountants.

The company has grown significantly during the past two years and the amount of paperwork needing to be stored is taking over a large amount of space in the building. The Senior Partner has decided that it would be a good idea to discard all paper-based records.

So, with little preparation, items of post are now scanned on receipt and forwarded electronically to the appropriate partner or accountant. All communications are PC based and every member of staff uses a networked desktop computer. The system is inadequate to cope with the requirements of the new systems and is prone to constant breakdowns. This brings the whole office to a grinding halt until the one member of staff who is responsible for the computer hardware and software is able to fix the problem.

A good deal of grumbling is occurring because more and more members of staff are having to work late regularly to catch up on outstanding work after each computer network breakdown.

The Senior Partner is determined to carry on with this new innovative way of managing paper and files and as he is away a good deal does not see or hear the grumbles that are becoming a daily occurrence.

Task

1. What communication issues can you identify in the Phillips Accountancy case study?
2. How could the new system of storing documents on the computer network have been introduced more smoothly and effectively?
3. What actions now need to be taken in order to improve both the communication process and the morale of the staff?

3

Non-verbal communication and body language

NON-VERBAL COMMUNICATION

Non-verbal communication is communication that does not use the spoken word. Gestures, expressions and actions can speak a great deal louder than any words. A smile, a frown, remaining silent, turning your back, being late for a meeting, etc, all 'say' something without any words being uttered. These non-verbal signals say a great deal about an individual.

Sometimes gestures are unintentional and an individual may not realize what their actions are conveying to others. Non-verbal signals can contradict a verbal message. For instance, body language, attitude, facial expressions etc, can give signals that convey a different meaning to what is being said.

Being able to read non-verbal signals effectively can help us to understand a person's real feelings when perhaps their spoken word must conform to expected, courteous responses or norms of behaviour. Learning to read different situations helps us to interpret non-verbal communication and respond appropriately.

It is generally accepted that women are more perceptive than men and appear to have an innate ability to pick up non-verbal signals. Experts suggest that much of our basic non-verbal behaviour is learned and that the meaning of many gestures is determined by the culture in which we are raised.

THE NATURE OF NON-VERBAL COMMUNICATION

The nature of non-verbal communication (excluding drawings, diagrams etc) is divided into four main areas:

1. Body language (kinesics), which includes:

   - Facial expressions.
   - The use of gestures.
   - Posture, although this is difficult to interpret.

   Body language is involuntary and unconscious and offers subtle messages about the way that we feel. Dejected individuals tend to slump, hold their head low and shoulders down. When we frown, smile, look puzzled, dash about, we convey messages about our health, attitudes and understanding.

2. Space (proxemics):

   - This relates to 'personal space' – the relationship between individuals will dictate what is comfortable.
   - The size of someone's office, car, desk, etc, can convey the status of management, for example.

3. Senses, which include:

   - *Sight*, which helps us to observe a person's reaction as well as their appearance, clothes and habits. A tidy or disorganized workspace for example.
   - *Sounds*, not just words are heard. Sighing, laughing, sobbing, etc, help to convey a message in a certain way.
   - *Touch*, which can be interpreted as aggressive and an intrusion of personal space, or may be interpreted as a gesture of friendship or support.

- *Smell*: perfumes and after-shaves help formulate an impression/ image of an individual, as does a problem with BO for example.
- *Taste* can help us to make judgements about individuals. Drinking the 'wrong wine' with dinner or choice of clothing engender our taste preferences.

4. Time:

- Taking time to talk to someone helps to create a feeling of value and confidence in the individual.
- Timing of messages is crucial:
  - These must be given in adequate time to be useful.
  - They must not be too early so that they are forgotten.
  - They must not be too late so that they end up being useless to the recipient.
- If communications are too long and irrelevant, then these waste time.

BODY LANGUAGE

Body language relates to the non-verbal messages that individuals portray through gestures and body signals and concerns the signals we give out without actually speaking. These include:

- the way we stand and the way we walk;
- our hand gestures and handshake;
- our facial expression(s) and our eye contact.

Charles Darwin published his study of body language in 1872 in a book entitled *The Expression of the Emotions in Man and Animals*. Since that time, many studies have been carried out regarding body language and facial expressions. Researchers in the twentieth century recorded around 1 million non-verbal cues and signals.

The study of non-verbal communication and body language became more significant only in the last four decades of the twentieth century. Some surprising research carried out by Albert Mehrabian during the last century suggested that the impact of a message is conveyed:

- 7 per cent by verbal means (speaking);
- 38 per cent vocal – tone and inflection in the voice coupled with other sounds; and
- 55 per cent by non-verbal means – gestures, facial expressions and body language.

Other researchers have produced similar findings, suggesting that a message is transmitted:

- 80 per cent by *body language*;
- 7 per cent by *words*;
- 13 per cent by *pitch* and *tone of voice*;

with the majority concluding that gestures and non-verbal signals account for the major way a message is communicated and that for the most part, basic non-verbal behaviour is learned.

Some basic gestures

Gestures tend to occur without us realizing or thinking about them. Pointing and jabbing a finger in someone's face is one step away from punching someone on the nose. A jerk of the head, for instance, can convey a direction. Gestures can be conveyed by all parts of the body and these can be widely misinterpreted.

Smiling, scowling, frowning and anger are all communicated through gestures that are recognized worldwide. Nodding the head is also a universally accepted indication of meaning 'Yes' or confirming agreement, whilst shaking the head is again universally accepted as meaning 'No' or disagreeing with what is being said.

Some gestures are interpreted differently depending on culture. As an example, let's take the 'thumbs-up' gesture. In the United Kingdom, New Zealand and Australia, the interpretation of this gesture is the same and it has three meanings:

- It is an OK signal.
- It is used by hitch-hikers to thumb a lift.
- When jerked upwards it is an insult, which means 'up yours'.

In Greece, the thumbs-up gesture has a completely opposite meaning and it is interpreted differently in other countries too. It is important to understand which gestures are appropriate in the markets and cultures within which an organization operates.

Facial expression

We convey a great deal through facial expression. Involuntary signals such as muscle twitches and being flushed or pale can indicate an individual's true feelings. Wide, narrow, or closed eyes, for instance, can convey a good deal without any actual talking taking place. That is why it is important to maintain eye contact in any personal interactions. Without strong eye contact, it might be suggested that there is disinterest. Strong eye contact suggests intimacy and understanding.

Posture

Decisions about whether to sit or stand and how you do these convey an involuntary message. Do you lounge in a chair? This can be interpreted as boredom, indifference or disinterest. Do you slouch when you are standing? This can suggest feelings of inferiority or laziness. Sitting or standing next to someone indicates a cooperative approach, whilst standing opposite to someone might be construed as being confrontational.

How close we stand or sit next to someone can have an impact on him or her. Invasion of what is perceived to be one's own space can be threatening. For example, if a salesperson steps onto your front doorstep when you open the door, this can create a feeling of invasion of personal space. In work environments, people tend to treat their table and chair as 'theirs' just as they will have their own cup or mug and their own place to sit in the staff restaurant. Someone else using his or her desk space or sitting in his or her perceived chair in the restaurant is treated as an invasion of personal space.

Touching or making contact can prove to be supportive or threatening. Slapping someone on the back implies that one is familiar and at ease with an individual, just as a helpful hand on the elbow to support or guide can also be perceived as supportive behaviour.

Other non-verbal clues

The movement or stillness of an individual can convey a good deal. Someone who is calm and self-possessed usually has stillness about him or her, whilst someone who moves without purpose can suggest that they are distracted or nervous. Walking briskly suggests determination and purpose.

Silence is often felt to be uncomfortable and sometimes an individual feels the need to fill the silence. Silence can feel embarrassing or awkward depending upon the circumstances and can also be difficult to interpret.

The personal appearance of an individual is a visual clue that creates first impressions. Someone who is attractive may well distract an interviewer from an interviewee's lack of intelligence and/or ability. How an individual is groomed and how they dress conveys an impression, which may be interpreted correctly or incorrectly. Style is very individual and instils self-confidence in the individual, as well as conveying individual taste and, sometimes, insecurity. Breaking norms relating to hygiene, dress and grooming can be interpreted as a direct challenge to authority or insensitivity in organizations where there is a culture of 'fitting in'. If behaviour and attitude do not fit within a specific context, the message being communicated is one of challenge, insensitivity, difference or possibly all three.

It is important not to interpret individual gestures in isolation. Just as sometimes it is necessary to write a complete sentence to convey meaning, it is also necessary to study a cluster of gestures to ensure that body language is correctly interpreted. It is also just as important to place into context the gestures being displayed.

There is a direct correlation between an individual's command of the spoken word and the amount of body language used. In the case of someone who is in a position of power, with the resulting prestige and status afforded to that individual, he/she would usually have a wide vocabulary and their use of body gestures and non-verbal communication would be limited. However, where an individual does not have a wide vocabulary, they are likely to make more use of hand gestures and body language to assist them in conveying their message.

BODY LANGUAGE AND BEHAVIOUR

Specific types of behaviour display different kinds of body language. Once familiar signals are identified, reading the attitude, stance and mood of an individual becomes easier.

Aggressive behaviour

Aggressive people tend to bring out negative feelings in everyone who encounters them. They can display a variety of non-verbal gestures and body language, which can be interpreted as being threatening:

- a stiff and rigid posture;
- standing very still with feet slightly apart;
- unwavering eye contact while shouting;
- arms folded across the chest;
- finger pointing/stabbing while speaking;
- thumping the table or desk;
- standing with hands on hips and leaning forward;
- coming very close to your face whilst speaking;
- always manoeuvring into a position of superior height.

Task

Do you, or does anyone you know, display all or some of the elements of aggressive behaviour? If so, what action, if any, do you propose to take?

Submissive behaviour

Individuals who display submissive behaviour tend to use non-verbal signals and body language, which includes:

- hunched shoulders and a stooped posture;
- speaking with a whining tone of voice;
- always looking down at the ground and avoiding eye contact;
- taking a step backwards when being spoken to;
- biting fingernails;
- wringing hands or twisting fingers together.

Assertive behaviour

Assertive people do display more relaxed body language and have a positive approach. Individuals who are assertive usually achieve their goals and the non-verbal signals and body language associated with assertiveness are:

- an upright, yet relaxed posture;
- a sense of calmness and composure;
- an ability to maintain eye contact without actually staring unwaveringly;
- always having a ready smile;
- hands and arms in open gestures;
- leaning slightly towards you while speaking in a friendly way.

Some approaches to using assertiveness in everyday situations at work are identified in the section below. In Table 3.1 the spoken word, non-verbal signals and body language are combined for submissive, assertive and aggressive behaviour, to give a summary overview.

Assertiveness in everyday situations

Making requests

- Be direct.
- Don't apologize profusely for needing information, documents etc.
- Keep it short.
- Give a reason for needing information if this helps – but keep it brief.
- Avoid manipulative language, flattery, playing on friendship or good nature.
- Don't take refusal personally.

Refusing requests

- Acknowledge the person requesting the information.
- Keep it short but not abrupt.
- Don't apologize profusely for not meeting requests.
- Give a reason if this helps.
- Honestly state the limitations and/or possibilities.
- Ask for clarification, if needed.
- Ask for more time to meet the request.
- Use non-verbal behaviour to avoid abruptness.

Giving criticism

- Check the motives.
- Check the facts.
- Give reasons.
- Be specific.

Table 3.1 Verbal and non-verbal signals

	Submissive	Assertive	Aggressive
Voice	Sometimes uncertain Tone may be whining Over soft or over warm Often dull and in monotone Quiet, often drops away at end	Steady and firm Tone is middle range, rich and warm Sincere and clear Not over loud or quiet	Very firm Tone is sarcastic, sometimes cold Hard and sharp Strident, may shout or voice rises at the end of a sentence
Speech Pattern	Hesitates and is full of pauses Sometimes shifts unexpectedly from fast to slow Frequent throat clearing	Fluent, few awkward pauses Emphasizes key words Steady, even pace	Fluent, few, if any pauses Often abrupt, clipped Often fast
Facial Expression	'Ghost' smiles when expressing anger, or being criticized Eyebrows raised in anticipation Quick changing features	Smiles when pleased Frowns when angry otherwise 'open' Features steady, not uncertain Jaw relaxed	Smile may become 'wry' Scowls when angry Eyebrows raised in amazement and/or disbelief Chin thrust forward
Eye Contact	Evasive Looking down	Firm but not fixed stare	Tries to stare down and dominate
Body Movements	Hand wringing Hunched shoulders Steps back Covers mouth with hand Nervous movements (shuffles and shrugs) to distract Arms crossed low for protection	Open hand movements Sits upright or relaxed (no slouching or cowering) Stands with head held up	Finger pointing Fist thumping Sits upright or leans forward Stands upright, head in the air Strides around impatiently Arms crossed high, meaning unapproachable

- Get a response.
- Listen actively.
- Ask for suggestions
- Summarize suggestions and actions.

Receiving criticism

- Listen actively.
- Evaluate what you are hearing.
- Avoid defending until you are clear of the facts.
- Establish facts – specific examples.
- Separate content of criticism from personal attack.
- Work on content – is it justified/unjustified?
- Look for solutions/progress.
- Suggest future actions.
- Use non-verbal behaviour – keep voice and eye contact steady.

Body language and non-verbal signals and gestures are a crucial element of all face-to-face communications. What we say is affected by how we say it and by the body language we display. Non-verbal communication leads us to erect or destroy barriers and make judgements. Body language and non-verbal gestures can replace, modify or change the meaning of the spoken word. It is a useful tool in interpreting all face-to-face interactions and communication.

Task

1. Review the body language that is displayed by assertive, aggressive and submissive behaviour.
2. Consider two or three individuals that you know well. Try to identify which type of body language each displays. Make sure that your assessment is objective and honest.

Task

1. Produce a list of the body language displayed by aggressive, assertive and submissive people – make sure you remove the headings.
2. Working with a colleague whom you know well and whose judgement you trust, ask them to identify any specific body language that you display from those listed.
3. Look at the list yourself and identify the body language you think you might display.
4. Compare the list you produce with the list produced by your colleague. Do they differ significantly?
5. Do you need to adjust your behaviour to ensure that you display different but appropriate body language in the future?

Scenario – non-verbal communication

Occasionally, we might feel that something we are hearing just doesn't sound quite right. We can't quite put our finger on why we feel this way but we know that what we are being told just doesn't ring true. This is usually because what is being said does not correlate with the body language being displayed. We usually talk about 'a gut feeling' being the reason why we don't truly believe what is being said.

Task

Consider a recent meeting or circumstance where the above might have occurred. What, if anything, did you do to clarify the situation?

4

Interviews

Within the remit of most managers, and more specifically for those managers who operate within an organization's human resource team, there is a need to be able to interview effectively, sometimes in a variety of contexts. The interview is a meeting that is arranged for a specific purpose.

Areas of operation that require management to possess appropriate interview skills include:

- the recruitment and selection process;
- interviews to assess the promotional potential of an individual;
- interviews as part of the appraisal process;
- disciplinary and grievance interviews;
- counselling interviews, which may relate to either personal or work-related issues;
- general fact-finding interviews, particularly in relation to absence investigation and accident investigation.

The interviewer must be in control of the interview to ensure that the objectives identified are achieved.

CHARACTERISTICS OF A GOOD INTERVIEWER

Ideally, the interviewer should possess and display a variety of traits. A good interviewer:

- is an ambassador for the organization and should be smartly dressed;
- should be serious-minded but at the same time good-humoured;
- should be self-disciplined and self-controlled;
- should be a good listener;
- should have a high degree of patience and be persistent;
- should be mentally agile and flexible;
- should be at ease in awkward situations;
- should be tolerant and understanding.

This list is not exhaustive, but it identifies the types of qualities a good interviewer should possess. It is unlikely that all managers who carry out interviews will possess all of the traits identified in the above list. It is important to remember that no one is perfect. However, all of us have some of these characteristics, and, with practice, it is possible to develop others.

Good interviewers encourage others to talk, have a tendency to be thoughtful and a little introspective, but are also able to be tough-minded when circumstances require it. Those who can be easily manipulated by others do not make good interviewers.

It is admirable to possess a sense of empathy or feeling for others, but too much sympathy for an individual can lead the interviewer into difficulties and away from the subject of the interview. This is particularly true when dealing with grievance or disciplinary interviews.

An interviewer needs to be conscientious and spend time collating information about those to be interviewed. Relevant facts should be gathered together, and issues that need clarification should be identified. It is important to work out what questions are to be asked prior to the interview taking place.

The ability to be patient is helpful when handling awkward situations. This ensures that the interviewer is able to be flexible and is also able to respond quickly to the unexpected without becoming flustered.

Task

Review the list of traits required in a good interviewer:

1. Be honest and objective and identify how many of these you currently possess.
2. Which traits do you need to improve or develop to ensure that your future performance in an interview situation is stronger than is currently the case?
3. What strategy will you adopt?

TWO MAIN INTERVIEW APPROACHES

Structured interviews

This approach adopts a very strict process. The questions that will be asked during the course of the interview are carefully formulated prior to the interview taking place. During the course of the interview, the interviewer will depart from those questions only occasionally, perhaps to clarify an issue or statement. In highly structured interviews, even the choice of answers expected from an interviewee may have been worked out in advance.

Structured interviews are mainly used in recruitment interviewing and are often adopted to ensure equal opportunity is afforded to all applicants.

Unstructured interviews

In unstructured interviews it is usual for the interviewer to have defined the objectives to be achieved during the interview process, ahead of the interviews actually taking place. Some questions may have been worked out beforehand but there is freedom to change the order in which they are asked and also to generate additional questions during the interview itself. The interviewee will be encouraged to do most of the talking, with the interviewer guiding the interview, using probing questioning techniques, and clarifying and summing up as the interview progresses.

Most management interviews tend to use a mixture of both the structured and unstructured approaches, adopting appropriate questioning techniques in each case.

Task

Is the approach you use when interviewing very structured or unstructured?

1. a) Do you have a clear plan, ie, introduce yourself and explain each stage of the interview process? Or,
   b) Do you plough in, with no clear direction and no real clue about what information you need to find out, what questions you should ask and with no strategy for making notes?
2. Do you need to improve your approach? If 'Yes', what exactly do you need to do?

TEN-POINT INTERVIEW CHECKLIST

Prior to any interview taking place, the following issues should be considered:

1. Have you defined the purpose of the interview?
2. Have you studied the relevant paperwork thoroughly? In the case of a recruitment interview, this might be the candidate's application form. In the case of an accident investigation, this might be the witness statements etc.
3. Have you decided on the main questions you will ask and the order in which you will ask them? In other words, have you decided on your strategy?

4. Are most of your questions open questions? These usually start with one of the following: **Who What Where When Why How**.
5. If this is a recruitment interview, does the waiting room look comfortable and relaxing? Have you provided some company literature for candidates to read?
6. Have you arranged the furniture in the interview room to encourage effective communication?
7. Is the room you are using free from distractions, ie, machinery noise, glare from the sun etc?
8. Have you made sure that you will not be interrupted during the interview?
9. Do you have the right documentation? The application letter/curriculum vitae/application form or the grievance/discipline documentation for instance?
10. Have you made sure that you know how to pronounce the interviewee's name?

When an interview is conducted in an appropriate way, it is an exchange of information between the interviewer and the interviewee. Each will have an agenda and there will be a need to change or adapt the interview approach based on information gleaned and feedback given.

Interviews require a wide range of communication skills, particularly in cases where there is a need to probe for information or persuade or discipline an individual. An interviewer needs to have the ability to:

- listen actively;
- interpret the interviewee's body language and use appropriate body language in return;
- recognize bias, attitudes and underlying implications by interpreting tone of voice and other inflections in the interviewee's speech;
- be diplomatic and persuasive and put others at ease;
- use appropriate questioning techniques and be enthusiastic, sympathetic etc, as appropriate.

THE INTERVIEW PROCESS

The following relate to all interview situations, whether these are for recruitment, fact-finding, or for some other purpose.

Preparation

The objectives of the interview must be identified and a framework for the interview should be developed. Relevant information will need to be gathered and analysed prior to the interview taking place. This is particularly relevant in the case of discipline, grievance or appraisal interviews.

The ergonomics of the environment in which the interview(s) take place will need to be considered and furniture organized to facilitate effective communication.

Conducting the interview

At the beginning of the interview, the purpose of the interview should be stated, except where recruitment interviews are concerned. The manner in which the interview is conducted will be apparent from the atmosphere and tone of communication adopted by both the interviewer and the interviewee.

It is crucial that the interviewer asks appropriate questions and listens carefully to the answers being given. The pace of the interview will need to be controlled by the interviewer. A range of appropriate questioning techniques should be adopted (see Chapter 1).

The interviewer must evaluate responses and make a judgement about what the interviewee may be trying to say or may be trying to cover up. Some individuals will have difficulty expressing themselves, whilst others will be reticent on purpose in order to avoid giving negative information. The interviewer needs to be selective and objective in evaluating the information he/she is hearing. Assessing the non-verbal clues, such as body language and gestures will assist in interpretation.

Closing the interview

It is helpful to summarize information to ensure that objectives set have been achieved and to identify whether any follow-up action is required. Clarification of understanding of any outcome should be sought and the meeting should be brought to a close courteously no matter what the outcome.

Follow-up

After the interview the interviewer should consider and assimilate all the information gained during the course of the exchange. Action required will need to be decided and notes should be made to ensure that an accurate record is kept on file. Any actions agreed or required should be initiated without delay.

Task

1. Where would you normally carry out a recruitment interview?
2. Is the environment appropriate?
3. If not, try to identify an appropriate location, that will prove to be a more appropriate venue for any interviews in the future.

Task

Consider your current approach to recruitment interviews.

1. What actions do you currently take to prepare ahead of the interview(s) taking place?
2. Are there strategies that you need to adopt to improve your ability to interview more effectively?

Case study: Fabrizio Fireworks Ltd

You are the Personnel Manager at Fabrizio Fireworks Limited. The company manufactures fireworks but has also developed a subsidiary company, which organizes firework displays at concerts, gala events etc.

The events aspect of the business is relatively new, having been operational for only five years. However, during that time, the business has developed a strong reputation for providing spectacular firework displays as well as a safe environment for both audience and company employees. Events are staged nationwide and due to the rapid expansion of this side of the business, Fabrizio Fireworks now needs to recruit an Operations Manager who will take responsibility for the events side of the business.

Task

Having short-listed six applicants for the post of Operations Manager, consider how you will approach the interviews for this post.

1. What actions will you take to prepare for these interviews?
2. Will the interviews be structured or unstructured?
3. Produce a list of questions that you will wish to ask each candidate.
4. Will other members of the management team be involved in the interview process?
5. What do you need to do to ensure that your interview skills are strong and appropriate?
6. Review your proposals.
7. Is there room for improvement? If so, what would you change?

Part 2

Interview processes

5

Job analysis, design of work and exit interviews

Job analysis is the process of examining a job to break it down into its component parts and identify the circumstances in which it is performed. This is to determine the essential characteristics of the job. The process involves gathering data to decide how jobs will need to be designed/re-designed and what specific skills, knowledge and experience are needed for both the current and future needs of the business.

Following the process of job analysis, a *job description* and/or *job specification* as well as a *personnel specification* will be produced for each job within an organization.

JOB ANALYSIS

Job analysis usually takes place when a job becomes vacant, or when a pay structure is being revised, or when targets are being identified. Analysis may take the form of observation for manual, repetitive jobs but for jobs where thinking skills come into play, such as people management, planning, etc, interviews and discussions with supervisors and the people concerned will be necessary.

Job analysis involves gathering information using both a task- and worker-orientated approach. The type of information sought includes:

- *Duties/responsibilities of the job* – materials required; equipment needed; identification of routine tasks; the level of difficulty, etc.
- *Employee requirements* – what qualifications are required; what level of experience is needed; what aptitudes are needed; what are the training requirements, etc.
- *Environment* – what are the hours of work; is a shift-work system in operation; what are the benefits; holiday periods; the quality of the physical environment; any hazards, etc.
- *Social aspects of the work* – is there a need for teamwork or are tasks/activities the responsibility of an individual; what level of personnel will the individual interact with, eg, management for instance; what is the status of the job, etc.

The following then is a brief reminder of the main elements of the job analysis process:

- *Job analysis* is the process of analysing a job to identify each of its component parts and the circumstances under which it is performed.
- A *job description* is a document that details a statement of the purpose, duties and responsibility of a specific job.
- A *job specification* is a detailed statement of the physical and mental activities that comprise the job and, when relevant, physical and social matters, such as the need for teamwork.
- A *personnel specification* interprets the job specification into terms that identify the personal attributes required of the person who will carry out the job.

Human resource audit

A human resource audit should also be carried out to facilitate the development of a *human resource plan*. A human resource audit results in the organization producing a document that identifies and lists the abilities, performance records and apparent potential of each department and its personnel.

The aim of a human resource audit is to match the present and future human resource needs of the organization against its current forecast requirements. The audit should identify the following:

- Jobs that will be newly created in the future; current jobs that will disappear in the future; current jobs that will be changed because of the need to re-design these. A time-line, which identifies when these changes will occur, should also be identified.
- An indication of the extent of redeployment that is possible or retraining that is required in relation to the current workforce.
- Identification of changes that will be necessary at supervisory and other management levels.
- Identification of training needs, again with an indication of time-scale.
- Recruitment, retirement and/or redundancy programmes.
- An indication of industrial relations issues that are likely to occur.
- Arrangements for feedback should modifications to the company plan or objectives be necessary.
- Details of arrangements for handling human resource problems that may arise from either a deficit or surplus of labour resulting from early retirement, rationalization of the workforce, etc.

Task

Does your organization use the process of job analysis to develop job descriptions and personnel specifications?

1. If 'Yes', compare the process you use with that described above. How does your process differ? How could you change your process to improve the outcome?
2. If 'No', take your own job as an example and carry out a job analysis exercise on it using the process described in this chapter.

JOB DESIGN

Job design is concerned with the shape and content of new posts or the re-design of existing ones – the latter usually following the introduction of a change to working practices, for instance. Design of jobs should create variety, autonomy and responsibility and instil motivation within the individual.

Job design is the process of deciding which tasks and responsibilities should be undertaken by particular employees. Design of work should also include consideration of methods, systems and procedures for completing the work. Job design is concerned with:

- patterns of accountability within the organization;
- spans of supervisory and management control; and
- interpersonal relations between colleagues.

The purpose of good job design is to stimulate the interest and involvement of employees, which motivates the individual to work that bit harder on behalf of the organization. Jobs may also be enlarged or enriched.

Job enlargement

Job enlargement involves increasing the scope of the job by extending the range of duties and responsibilities inherent within it. The intention is to motivate the individual by reversing the process of specialization. Specialization, by its very nature, restricts the activities of the individual. By enlarging an individual's role, it allows flexibility, multi-skilling, multi-tasking and growth, which creates interest and motivates employees.

Job enrichment

Job enrichment seeks to allocate more interesting, challenging and possibly more difficult duties, which in turn stimulate an individual's sense of participation and concern for achieving both the company's and their own individual objectives. Individuals achieve a sense of ownership and are more motivated to seek to continually improve their performance.

Job enrichment entails:

- offering an individual scope for more decision-making;
- facilitating involvement in activities that require higher level skills than are currently required – analytical, strategic and project management skills, for instance;
- possibly having greater contact with customers and/or suppliers, both internal and external to the organization;
- being responsible for the quality of an individual's work;
- requiring more discretion about how an individual will go about achieving their own objectives and, ultimately, those of the organization.

Job extension

Job extension embraces both job enlargement and job enrichment. It is considered that a wide variety of tasks lead an individual to realize the significance of their role within the wider context of the organization as a whole. This, in turn should result in a more contented and productive individual.

QUALITY OF WORKING LIFE

Job extension is considered crucial in any development programme that seeks to improve the quality of working life for employees. It has been suggested that by adopting this approach, every employee will achieve total satisfaction at work. It will be necessary for any organization that decides to adopt this approach to consider a number of issues:

- To what extent will employees be involved in the decision-making process? If little or none, careful consideration will be needed in the re-design of working practices.

■ What is the quality of the working environment provided by the organization? Is the environment clean and safe and is equipment regularly maintained and technology up-to-date?

■ What are the values and beliefs that are engendered within the organization's culture?

■ Is the organization structured in a way that facilitates effective interpersonal and inter-group relations within it, particularly in relation to quick and effective communication systems?

■ What style of management is inherent within the organization? Is the approach one that is threat-centred and that engenders bullying and harassment? Or, is there already a participative approach, with individuals being encouraged to be involved in the decision-making process?

■ What is the level of stress experienced by individual workers? Does the company have a high incidence of absence, more particularly, sickness absence?

JOB DESCRIPTION

A job description describes the job at a particular moment in time and identifies the specific tasks to be performed. It does exactly what it says – it describes the job.

Jobs tend to be dynamic and change regularly, particularly in the current business climate. It is important therefore that job descriptions are updated regularly.

Purposes of a job description

A job description is a useful tool that can be used for a variety of purposes. These include:

1. In recruitment, to identify:
   - the skills and qualifications required by the post-holder;
   - the main duties of the post-holder;
   - a fair rate of pay, which is on a par with competitors.

2. In job evaluation, when it is used to set levels of pay:

   - a standard format facilitates job comparison;
   - a job description is focused on the job not the job-holder;
   - job-holders and managers can discuss differences about what the job involves.

3. In induction training – it is useful to help new employees to understand their role.
4. It is useful in identifying overlaps in work and therefore assists in helping to structure the organization more effectively.

Content of a job description

A job description would usually include the following information:

1. **Job title**.
2. **Department** in which the job 'sits'.
3. **Supervisor** – the person to whom the job-holder reports, ie, the line manager.
4. **Salary grade** if a salary scale exists within the organization.
5. **Summary of the job** – one or two sentences that describe, in general terms, the scope of the post and its purpose.
6. **Duties or job content**. In the case of a management role, a list of the main duties of the role. In the case of a manual job, the sequence of operations that make up the job.
7. **Responsibility for**. An indication of how many staff, if any, the job-holder is responsible for.
8. **Hours of work** – and details of any shift-working arrangements.
9. **Names and positions** held by people who have drawn up the document.
10. **The date** when the document was prepared.

An example of a job description for a Personnel Officer is shown in Figure 5.1.

THE REALLY USEFUL GARMENT CO

Job Description

Job Title: Personnel Officer
Location: Head Office, Swindon
Responsible To: Human Resources Manager
Responsible For: 1 secretary
                        3 clerical assistants
Salary: Scale 10–15

Purpose of Post:
To assist the Human Resources Manager with the recruitment and selection process.

Key Duties:
1. To take responsibility for recruitment and selection of all non-management clerical personnel.

   1.1   Write job descriptions and personnel specifications in line with company policy.

   1.2   To produce and place relevant advertisements and monitor effectiveness.

   1.3   Make arrangements for recruitment interviews.

   1.4   Represent the Human Resources Department on recruitment interview panels as required.

   1.5   Take up references and produce and forward offer letters.

2. To maintain personnel records and monitor applications in line with relevant legislation.

3. To prepare contracts of employment and issue as appropriate.

4. To create and maintain relevant personnel records.

5. To advise payroll of details of new employees.

6. To organize induction training for all non-management clerical personnel.

7. To supervise three clerks and one secretary in the Human Resources Department.

8. To take responsibility for special projects and other duties as allocated from time to time by the Human Resources Manager.

9. Hours of work will be as per terms and conditions of employment, although it may be necessary to work overtime from time to time to ensure satisfactory completion of duties.

Last Updated (date):_____

Produced by (name(s):_____

Designation(s): _____

Figure 5.1   An example of a job description for a Personnel Officer

Task

1. Design a master job description document, based on the main headings identified in Figure 5.1 above, which you propose to use within your organization.
2. Use this document to produce a job description for either a management or manual post within your organization. Include as much information as is relevant within this document.
3. Evaluate the job description layout and content by discussing these with relevant individuals within your organization. Make adjustments as appropriate.
4. Develop a proposal for your line manager, which supports the adoption of this method of identifying roles to assist in the retention of current staff and the recruitment of personnel in the future.

PERSONNEL SPECIFICATION

A personnel specification is a document that is designed to identify the knowledge, skills and personal attributes/characteristics required of an individual in a specific role. The document is used as part of the recruitment process to enable the appointment of the most appropriate individual to a specific post. The personnel specification should also identify the competencies required, particularly if the recruitment process is to be competence-based.

The specific attributes are usually identified as either 'Essential' or 'Desirable'. In drawing up any personnel specification, legal issues relating to equal opportunities should be taken into account and the document can then be used as a basis for advertising the vacancy. The specification is intended to describe the person who would be best suited to carry out the job.

Content of a personnel specification

A personnel specification would usually contain the following information:

1. **Job title**
2. **Experience**:

   - previous posts (whether full- or part-time);
   - work experience;
   - sandwich course work placements (Higher National Diploma/ Degree programmes);
   - voluntary work etc.

3. **Personality**:

   - confident;
   - self-starter;
   - discretion/tact;
   - sense of humour etc.

4. **Physical characteristics**:

   - manual dexterity;
   - vision;
   - hearing etc.

5. **Qualifications**:

   - Degree/Masters;
   - professional qualification(s);
   - NVQs
   - 'A' levels/vocational qualifications;
   - GCSEs.

6. **Interests/hobbies**:

   - languages, sport, computer skills etc.

7. **Circumstances**:

   - availability;
   - flexibility;
   - clean driving licence etc.

An example of a personnel specification for a Personnel Officer is detailed in Figure 5.2.

THE REALLY USEFUL GARMENT CO

Personnel Specification

Job Title: Personnel Officer

Criteria	Essential	Desirable
1. Experience	At least one year's experience of recruitment and personnel administration. Demonstrate computer literacy and ability to use Microsoft Office Suite.	At least one year's experience of supervising staff. Knowledge of current employment law. Able to carry out job analysis and draw up JD and PS. Able to design advertisements and organize induction training.
2. Personality	Strong interpersonal skills Conscientious and able to see tasks through to completion. Confident self-starter.	None
3. Physical characteristics	20:20 corrected vision	None
4. Qualifications	Degree	CPP/IPD qualification IT Level 2 qualification
5. Interests/Hobbies	None	None
6. Circumstances	Clean driving licence Flexible approach to work.	None

Figure 5.2   An example of a personnel specification for a Personnel Officer

Task

Produce a job description and personnel specification for one or more of the following:

1. A Personal Assistant for a Managing Director;
2. A Marketing or Sales Manager;
3. A Supervisor for a company's production line;
4. A trainee Clerical Assistant;
5. A Forklift Truck Driver;
6. A Manager for one of a number of clothing retail outlet branches.

JOB SATISFACTION

Job satisfaction is concerned with considering how favourably an employee views their work role. Individuals who are very satisfied with their role will be cooperative and well motivated. They will also see a strong correlation between the rewards they expect to receive for carrying out their role efficiently, effectively and successfully, and those that are actually provided by the organization.

Dissatisfied employees will be more inclined to be absent from work regularly, and produce poor quality work. They are also likely to be more inclined to invoke the grievance procedure, or may even go on strike. Ultimately, it is likely that they will leave the organization. This would be unfortunate for the organization if the individual in question possessed skills that were in short supply, both within the current workforce and also in the wider external labour market.

Factors that affect job satisfaction include:

- *Performance* – high performance may in itself result in job satisfaction because the achievement of stiff targets can generate a sense of achievement, which may also result in greater financial reward. However, if the rewards are perceived by an individual to be inadequate then this will create dissatisfaction.
- *Group working/interpersonal relationships* – employees who are an integral part of a group and who support its objectives and norms of behaviour are usually very satisfied with their job.
- *Quality of supervision* – it is usual to find high levels of job satisfaction where managers use a participative, employee-centred leadership approach.
- *Content of the job* – work should be varied, challenging and interesting to result in high levels of job satisfaction. It has been argued that even the most basic task can be made interesting and enjoyable.
- *Pay and working conditions* – reward systems should reflect the level and complexity of the work. A package, which includes a mixture of basic pay, performance-related bonus, and other benefits, needs to be considered. The working environment affects the physical comfort of an employee. High levels of job satisfaction are found where an appropriately safe and clean working environment is provided for all employees and where equipment is up-to-date

and well maintained. Job satisfaction is also high when appropriate consideration has been given to the provision of welfare facilities such as café/restaurant facilities, rest rooms, etc.

▪ *Job status* – the higher the status of the role the more an employee's job satisfaction is increased. This does not solely relate to the level achieved within the organization's hierarchy but can often relate to specialist skills and/or knowledge, which are in short supply in the workforce generally.

▪ *Effective communications* – communication systems within organizations are often the main source of dissatisfaction. Where communication systems break down and effective communication is lacking, individuals become frustrated and feel that they are unable to bring any influence to bear on their working life.

JOB DISSATISFACTION

Job dissatisfaction is evident when a number of issues become apparent. For instance, where there is a:

▪ high rate of staff turnover;
▪ high level of absenteeism;
▪ high number of grievances.

In an organization affected by any or all of the above, a job satisfaction survey may highlight some of the issues that need to be addressed by management. Job satisfaction surveys are useful to:

▪ identify any sources of low morale;
▪ assist in identifying the levels of satisfaction between different groups of workers, ie, different departments, male and female employees, specific roles etc;
▪ afford an opportunity to improve communication between management and the workforce and provide opportunities for employees to express their views;
▪ assess the impact of the organization's policies on the workforce.

Questionnaires and/or interviews are usually used in such surveys and questions may well be open-ended in order to gather as much information as is feasible.

Task

You are to act as Human Resource Manager for your own organization.

1. Consider the information you will need to gather to assist you in assessing the levels of satisfaction/dissatisfaction within your own organization.
2. Design a proposed questionnaire for use in carrying out a survey of the whole workforce.
3. Identify the process you propose, which will be used to analyse and facilitate the production of strategic proposals based on the outcome of the analysis.

EXIT INTERVIEWS

Many organizations now seek information regarding why people leave. Some organizations also carry out 'exit interviews', which allows them to gather data that may prove useful in future planning. However, there are still a large number of organizations that do not carry out such interviews.

Interviewing employees who have decided to leave the organization can provide an employer with a good deal of valuable information. Employees who are leaving tend to be more forthcoming with their opinions regarding, for instance, problems with managers/supervisors, morale, the content of the job, etc. This kind of information is useful to an organization, particularly if there is a high level of staff turnover. Gathering information, which will assist the organization to improve both the environment and the work, will ultimately result in retention of good employees and can only be beneficial to the organization in the long run.

EXIT INTERVIEW REPORT

Name:_____ Staff No: _____

Department and Location: _____

Position held: _____

Start date: _____ Salary: _____

Termination date: _____

The employee:

Resigned	
Retired	
Was dismissed	
Other	

Reason(s) for termination (in cases of dismissal):

Interviewer's comments:

Is re-employment recommended? Yes/No

If 'No', please state reasons.

Signed:_____ Date:_____

Designation:_____

Figure 5.3   An example of an Exit Interview Report Form

Figure 5.3 gives one example of an Exit Interview Report Form that could be used for the purpose of exit interviews. It is usual for the individual's line manager to carry out such interviews. However, if there have been problems between the individual and their immediate line manager, it may be more appropriate for the manager responsible for personnel issues to undertake the interview.

Exit interviews should be carried out as soon as possible after it is known that the employee is leaving. If the employee is valued, it is likely that any attempt to persuade them to stay would be more successful if approached during the course of the exit interview. Morale of employees can be improved if members of staff feel that the employer cares enough to want to know the reasons for their resignation and that this information is being sought quickly.

Why people leave organizations

Some of the reasons for leaving, which have been identified by organizations that do carry out exit interviews, are included below. The reasons given for leaving by employees are diverse and make interesting reading:

- *work-related* – leaving voluntarily because working conditions are 'hard' or 'dirty'; hours are difficult, 'always on nights'; poor pay; better job somewhere else; 'supervisor's always on at me'; lack of training and/or support; pressure of work; disillusioned; 'job isn't what I was expecting';
- *non-work related* – leaving voluntarily because needed a job but couldn't find anywhere affordable to live; no transport; domestic problems; took early retirement; health problems;
- *legal* – leaving involuntarily because: made redundant; dismissed.

If there is a high rate of staff turnover, the organization needs to find out why this is occurring. Issues to be addressed would include establishing whether:

- morale or motivation is low;
- working conditions are deemed to be poor;
- pay structures are unsuitable;
- other incentives, including performance-related bonuses, merit awards etc, should be given where these currently do not apply;
- recruitment and selection policies may need to be revised.

Task

Consider your own organization:

1. Are exit interviews carried out as a matter of course when an employee hands in their notice?
2. If 'Yes', how effective are these in identifying underlying trends for dissatisfaction within the workforce?
3. If 'No', consider the type of information that would be needed to assist your organization in better retention of staff.
4. Design a process, with documentation, which will form part of a proposal for your Human Resource Manager.

Case study: The Supreme Insurance Co Ltd

The Supreme Insurance Co Ltd has a large head office based in the West Midlands, which provides centralized services and management support for its many branches across the United Kingdom.

The computer support department consists of approximately 150 staff, mainly analysts and project managers but with some programmers. The department head is Donald Drucker who has apparently said that his department has so much work to do that new projects are off the agenda for the time being. He feels he couldn't possibly take on any further new initiatives.

Sarah Giles, who has worked in the computer support department for about 18 months and who is considered to be an extremely gifted analyst, has just handed in her notice.

When interviewed by the company's Personnel Officer, she has given her reasons for leaving as: 'I'm bored. I haven't had any work to do for the past two months.' She also feels that there is no sense of identity with either the company or with Donald Drucker whom she has never met, apparently, and isn't sure that she would recognize him even if she bumped into him.

Task

You are to take the role of the Human Resource Manager at The Supreme Insurance Co Ltd.

1. What implications does this case have regarding job analysis and job design?
2. Is adequate information available for you to be able to identify the actions you need to take?
3. If 'Yes', what would be your next step?
4. If 'No', how would you propose to gather adequate information in the future to enable you to identify relevant issues more effectively?

Case study: Felix Laboratories

Felix Laboratories is a small company that specializes in developing carbon matrix materials for use in a variety of industries where heat protection is crucial.

During the past two years the company has had to advertise the post of Head of Quality Assurance in the main laboratory a total of three times. Jim Brown is the most recent recruit and has been in post for just three months. He has just handed in his notice.

Jim's Department Manager, Roger Blake, just can't believe that this has happened again and has just walked into Faye Miller's office. Faye is the company's newly appointed Human Resource Manager.

'Faye, we've got a problem. Jim Brown's just handed in his notice. He's been with us for such a short period of time. I'm at a loss to know what to do next. We've appointed three people to the post of Head of Quality Assurance in the past two years and every time, after a brief period in the job, they've left.'

Faye dug out a copy of the job description and person specification for the post of Head of Quality Assurance and then turned to Roger.

'Tell me Roger, what is it that you expect the Head of Quality Assurance to do specifically?'

'Well, he or she needs to monitor the quality of the product and complete various reports, which are forwarded to the Operations Manager.'

Faye's next question was: 'Is there any research or development work attached to the post?'

'Well, no, not really. It's purely a monitoring role.'

Faye's next question was: 'Has anyone asked any of these individuals why they wanted to leave after such a short period with the company?'

Looking puzzled, Roger said, 'No, I don't think so – at least I certainly haven't.'

Faye scanned the job description and personnel specification and then said. 'You know, you're asking for extremely high-level qualifications and extensive product development experience, especially for a post that really is just for monitoring production.'

'Yes, but it's important, if we get the quality wrong, we'll lose contracts, but more importantly, someone could get badly hurt,' Roger said.

'I'm sure it is important and I take on board everything you've just said, but do you really need someone qualified to this level? To be honest, I'm not surprised people have left the job quickly. They were probably bored. The job description implies that the type of work involved will be complex and that elements of it relate to development processes. However, talking to you now, it suggests that's not quite the case. Am I right?' Faye asked.

'I suppose so,' Roger said 'but what do you suggest?'

Task

Put yourself in the role of Human Resource Manager at Felix Laboratories.

1. Identify the main issues that need to be addressed.
2. What strategies would you propose to improve the recruitment and retention of appropriate personnel to the post of Head of Quality Assurance?

6

Recruitment and selection

Businesses currently operate in an environment that is constantly changing. Whereas in the past change was developmental, the current nature of change is dynamic and unpredictable. It is likely that the skills, knowledge and attitude of individuals, whilst relevant now, may need to change next year to meet the ever-changing requirements of the organization.

It is crucial to consider not only the personal criteria that affect job performance but also the specific role and/or the demands made on individuals in different situations within the work environment. Experiences change people.

Recruitment involves the organization in activities that will result in:

- recruiting appropriate candidates for posts by being seen to use a process that is fair and equitable for all;
- the organization displaying an appropriate image and achieving company goals; and
- efficient and cost-effective recruitment and selection processes.

The organization's recruitment and selection processes should facilitate achievement of the organization's human resource plan. The section below identifies the data required to produce a staffing plan.

In addition, the recruitment and selection process should conform to the organization's equal opportunities policy. A company's image can be enhanced when it adopts the principles of being an equal opportunities employer. It is also likely that such an organization

---

EQUAL OPPORTUNITIES POLICY STATEMENT

The company is committed to providing a working environment in which employees are able to realize their full potential and contribute to business success irrespective of race, gender or disability.

The company is committed to identifying and eliminating any discriminatory attitudes, procedures and practices within the organization. Employees are expected to support these principles and apply them in practice.

The company aims to ensure that no employee or job applicant is discriminated against, whether directly or indirectly, on the grounds of gender, nationality, ethnicity, marital status, religion or disability. This commitment applies to all aspects of employment related to: recruitment and selection; training and development and appraisal; terms and conditions of employment; grievance and discipline; and redundancy.

The company will review its policy regularly in line with revisions in Equal Opportunities legislation to improve equality of opportunity within the organization.

Figure 6.1   An example of a company's Equal Opportunities Policy Statement

would be able to attract and retain staff who had been recruited from the widest selection available. An example of a company's Equal Opportunities Policy Statement appears in Figure 6.1. Equal opportunities policies, when used properly, provide a mechanism to avoid making decisions based on prejudice and offer all staff the opportunity to reach their full potential.

PRODUCING A STAFFING PLAN

The data that will be required to assist in producing a staffing plan is as follows.

Internal data

- the number of people leaving the organization, including the reasons for their leaving;
- the number of people known to be leaving, ie, those leaving because of retirement;
- the number of people joining the organization;
- the average length of time that people stay with the organization.

This information describes the labour turnover or rate of labour in an organization. A degree of labour turnover is generally considered to be both useful and desirable. This allows the organization to bring in 'new blood' and consequently new ideas. However, a high level of labour turnover is not desirable, as this can prove extremely costly in terms of:

- costs incurred in training new staff and the impact of the learning curve on efficiency levels;
- costs incurred in the recruitment and selection process;
- costs incurred when employees leave;
- higher costs incurred for existing staff who take on extra work to cover for vacant posts.

External data

Information needs to be gathered on issues that impact on an organization but that occur outside the organization and over which the organization has no control. These include:

- _Population_ – depending upon the size of the organization, studying trends in the population, ie, locally, regionally, nationally and increasingly internationally.
- _Economic conditions_ – changes in the economy have a direct effect on demand for products and this affects the demand for labour.

■ *Technological changes* – new materials, products and methods of work affect the demand for the type and number of employees needed.

Information needed for a staffing plan

Supply of labour depends on:

■ current staffing levels;
■ current skills available;
■ future skills needed;
■ output/productivity;
■ pay rates;
■ legal constraints;
■ economic environment.

Demand for labour depends on:

■ forecast sales;
■ forecast production;
■ past trends (to a lesser degree in the current dynamic business climate);
■ changes in technology;
■ reduction in labour needs;
■ legal constraints.

METHODS OF SELECTION

A variety of methods of selection are available to an employer, and it is the task of the organization to decide upon those methods that are likely to result in the appointment of the most appropriate candidate to fill the advertised vacancy. The methods chosen will invariably differ depending upon the type and level of post to be filled.

Choosing the right person for the job is critical to an organization's success. Methods of selection encompass an extensive range of options, which range from graphology to interviews to psychometric testing. The intention here is to focus on those methods that are most commonly used in recruitment.

The recruitment interview

The interview is just one element in the selection process, which aims to ensure that the organization recruits the individual who best meets the criteria for selection decided upon for a specific job role. The interview should be just one aspect of a wider process to ensure that selection is objective and that the best person for the job is selected.

Other selection methods could include:

- in-tray exercises;
- group/team activities;
- an oral presentation;
- work simulations;
- psychometric and other tests such as language, numeracy, etc;
- personality profiling.

Exactly how many selection methods are decided upon will depend upon the type and level of post the organization is looking to fill.

Recruitment and selection interviews are often carried out by managers and other individuals who have never been trained in the 'how to' of the interview. If the interviewer is unclear about what they are looking for, then an interview will not help in finding the most appropriate person for the job. Similarly, if the information gleaned at interview is used inappropriately, or if the individual does not know how to use the information collated, then the interview will have proved a useless exercise. Human Resource Managers can help to develop good practice within organizations, and arrange training and development for those managers who will be involved in interview processes in order to improve performance in this aspect of their role.

Interviews, more often than not, are carried out on a one-to-one basis. However, a sequential process may be used or, in certain more formal recruitment processes, a panel interview will be arranged.

Sequential interviews are in fact, a series of one-to-one interviews, each interviewer meeting with the candidate and asking questions relating to their area of operation/expertise. This method does not necessarily extend the interview process, but means that the interview time is split between the number of interviewers.

Panel interviews usually involve at least two and often up to a dozen interviewers. This approach is more formal and will need careful organization if the process is to prove successful. Often, with panel interviews, it is difficult for the candidate to know to whom they should address their answer. A panel interview process often makes the candidate(s) feel very uncomfortable.

As with any other type of interview, recruitment interviews need to take place in an appropriate environment. The room needs to be quiet with as few noise distractions as possible and interruptions should be avoided.

The way that candidates are initially met, and how they are dealt with during their period of time on company premises, will reflect on the organization itself. If the experience is positive for the individual then the chosen candidate is more likely to accept any offer of employment than if their experience has been one of chaos, delays and ill manners. The interview and selection process should be slick and professional and portray the professional image, values and culture to which the company aspires.

There are many 'dos' and 'don'ts' in the interview process but some of the more important ones are:

- Do allow the candidates to speak. The interviewer should speak for only 20 per cent or so of the time allocated. The intention is to find out as much as possible about a candidate. If the interviewer does most of the talking, it is likely that when the paperwork is reviewed, too little information will have been gleaned and the task of selection will prove to be impossible.
- Most interviewers make up their minds about a candidate within the first five minutes or so of meeting them. Normally, the paperwork that has been submitted by candidates 'sells' their individual

strengths to an organization. This is usually what makes the employer select an individual for interview. The interview then is just the process during which the employer is seeking to affirm that their initial perceptions were correct.

- It is often true that the last candidate to be seen is the one that is remembered more clearly than those that came before.
- Remember that less than 10 per cent of communication is by the spoken word, the remaining 90 per cent is by interpreting body language, tone of voice, accent etc. Therefore, non-verbal communication is important in interpreting what a candidate is saying.
- The interview is a marketing opportunity for the organization. It is an opportunity to 'sell' the organization to candidates.
- Whilst interviews are a relatively cheap method of selection, if the process is weak and the wrong candidate is selected, the need to re-advertise, interview and select for a second time is a costly exercise in terms of both time and money.
- Panel interviews are notoriously difficult when trying to reach a consensus about which candidate is the strongest. Often, the person who leads the panel will be able to exact significant influence over other members, which then negates the reason for holding a panel interview in the first place.
- The interview still remains the most popular method for selection. The main difficulties are with managers who have inadequate interview technique. It is important to know *how* to conduct an interview effectively. Less important is how long a manager may have been carrying out interviews. More important is whether a manager is adopting an appropriate interview technique. Regardless of whether a manager has been interviewing for one year or 20 years, if the manager's interview skills are inadequate, practice will not improve performance especially if the manager continues to use the same incorrect technique.

The traditional interview tends to suffer from being unstructured and can often be subject to bias on the part of the interviewer. There have been criticisms also in terms of equal opportunities. The response has been to try and ensure that the interview becomes more structured and prescribed.

The structured interview usually requires candidates to respond to a prescribed situation. Examples include:

- *Situational issues* – hypothetical situations are given to candidates who are asked to explain how they would react in a given situation.
- *Behavioural approach* – candidates are asked to identify situations where they experienced specific job-related issues. The interviewer then uses the probing technique to establish exactly what action the candidate took in each case.

These approaches have been shown to improve the validity of criteria-based assessment by being more job-related.

The interview process

There are a number of steps that make up the interview process. Each one is as important as the next to ensure that the appropriate candidate(s) is/are recruited to the organization.

Every interview has a purpose. The purpose of the recruitment interview is to find the right person for the right job at the right time.

Useful documentation

There are a number of documents that could prove useful in supporting the interview process.

Documents provided by the candidate   Those documents that would be produced by an applicant could include all, or just one of the following documents depending upon the approach being taken by the recruiting organization:

- *Curriculum vitae* – this document summarizes an individual's personal data together with educational and work experience information.

■ *Application form* – The data supplied will be as per the content requested on the form (see Figure 6.2 for a sample Application for Employment Form).

APPLICATION FOR EMPLOYMENT

Please complete in black ink or type
You may attach a Curriculum Vitae to this application form. However, please complete all sections of the form

Post Applied For:

How did you find out about this vacancy (please list media)

1. **Personal Details**

Surname/Family Name:	First Name(s): Title:
Address:	Home Tel No:
	Work Tel No:
Postcode:	Mobile No:
National Insurance No:	E-mail Address:
Date of Birth	Nationality:

2. **Present/Most Recent Employer**

Name of Employer:	Address:
Job Title:	
Start Date:	Postcode:
Date Left/Notice Period:	Current/Most Recent Salary:

3. **Profile**

Please provide a **summary** of relevant experience to date and state why you think you should be considered for this post.

Figure 6.2   An example of an Application for Employment Form

4. Qualifications

Starting with the highest, please list all qualifications, grades, institution and date acquired.

Qualification and Grade	Institution	Date

5. Education

Please list all educational establishments attended since age 11, starting with the most recent.

University/College/School	Dates Attended

6. Continuing Professional Development and Training

Please list any other training you would like us to consider in support of your application.

7. Membership of a Professional Body

Please list below membership of any professional institute(s) and state how long you have been a member.

Figure 6.2   continued

8. Health

I enjoy good health and am not aware of any medical condition that might give rise to a health problem in the future.

Signed: Date:

If you are unable to sign the above statement, please provide further details of your state of health.

Signed: Date:

9. Referees

Please give the name and contact details of two people who have agreed to act as referees on your behalf. One should be your current or most recent employer.

Title:	Address:
Name:	
Telephone No:	
E-mail:	Postcode:
Can we take this reference further without consultation with yourself? Yes/No	Relationship to you:

Title:	Address:
Name:	
Telephone No:	
E-mail:	Postcode:
Can we take this reference further without consultation with yourself? Yes/No	Relationship to you:

10.   Declaration

I confirm that the information provided above, and in any attachments, is correct and understand that any false statement could result in my application or appointment being terminated.

Signed: Date:

Please make sure that you have completed ALL sections of this application form.

Please forward completed form to: (Name and address to whom documents should be addressed)

Figure 6.2   continued

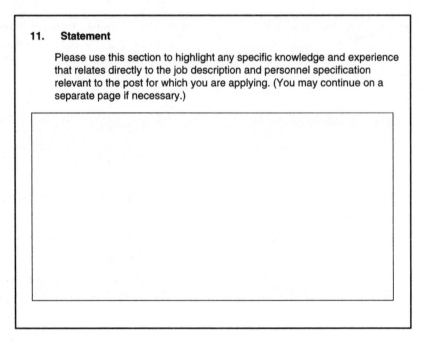

11.   Statement

Please use this section to highlight any specific knowledge and experience that relates directly to the job description and personnel specification relevant to the post for which you are applying. (You may continue on a separate page if necessary.)

Figure 6.2   continued

■ *Letter of application* – Most *white collar* posts, ie, administration or managerial, require the applicant to produce a letter of application, usually in addition to submitting an application form or curriculum vitae. The letter usually highlights those areas of expertise and experience that are relevant to the post for which the applicant is applying.

Task

Develop an appropriate application form that can be used for:

1. hourly paid workers, whether for part-time or full-time, permanent or temporary employment;
2. management and office staff, including supervisors employed on the production line;
3. personnel employed in a retail shop, whether management, checkout operators, shelf-fillers, warehouse operatives etc.

Documents produced by the organization Documentation that may prove useful and that would be produced by the organization to facilitate the interview process could include all, or some, of the following:

- *Job description* – detailing the main duties and responsibilities of a job.
- *Personnel specification* – detailing the individual attributes required for the post.
- *Advertisement* – which includes as much information as possible to facilitate the application process.
- *Organization chart or organizational/departmental information* – which would offer information about the organization, its structure and operation and identify where the post fits within the overall organization structure.
- *Assessment forms* – a form that allows scoring or other information to be recorded during the interview. Usually, these look at specific assessment areas that are key to the post.

Recruitment interviews offer the opportunity for both sides to gather as much information about each other as possible.

The applicant tries to establish that the terms and conditions of the post advertised match their expectations. They are likely to be seeking to establish whether there are opportunities for career development. They may also wish to look at the long-term prospects of the organization.

Organizations tend to be looking for confirmation that the person with whom they are having a one-to-one interview matches the information contained within the individual's written application.

Organizations increasingly use a variety of selection methods to establish attitudes to work and also the expertise and abilities of the individual. An individual's potential for future development is also usually assessed during the interview process.

A number of factors need to be considered to ensure that the recruitment interview process is effective and successful.

Preparing for the interview(s)

It is important to be fully prepared prior to the interview(s) taking place:

1. Find out as much information as possible about each candidate prior to the interviews taking place.
2. Analyse the application form or curriculum vitae as well as the letter of application for each candidate.
3. Make a note of the important questions you wish to ask before the interview begins.
4. It is important to make sure that there will be no interruptions during the course of an interview. Ensure that telephone calls are re-routed or messages taken and that staff understand that you are unavailable.
5. The interview room should be free from distractions.
6. The seating arrangements should be such that you and the candidate can see and hear each other clearly. Desks, tables and other pieces of furniture can act as barriers to communication. Comfortable chairs, positioned at right angles to each other have proved to be an effective arrangement.
7. It is important that candidates are comfortable and relaxed to aid effective communication.

On the day – the interview itself

The interview should follow a pre-organized process. For instance:

1. The interviewer should greet the candidates in a friendly, polite and open manner. If possible, the interviewer should step out of the interview room in order to meet each candidate.
2. Effective interviewers ask questions that allow the candidate to give a comprehensive answer. Using more open questioning techniques will facilitate this approach. The reason for the face-to-face interview is so that the interviewer can find out as much

information as possible about each candidate. There is only a brief time to do this. If the interviewer does most of the talking, they will realize, after the event, that they will have found out very little about the candidate over and above what has been submitted within the written application.

3. The interviewer should avoid asking too many closed questions that require only a one-word reply such as 'Yes' or 'No'. Closed questions are best used to tighten up understanding of an unclear response made by the candidate or to clarify specific information.

4. The candidates should do most of the talking, whereas the interviewer needs to show by voice, facial expression and gestures that they are listening actively to what the candidate is saying to them.

5. The interviewer should use appropriate questioning techniques to clarify any information that is unclear.

6. In view of the legislation that governs discrimination in the workplace, it is important to avoid all unnecessary and irrelevant references to the candidate's appearance, sex, age, religion or race.

7. There should be a clear structure to the interview and the interviewer should keep an eye on time. Adequate time should be allocated for each interview and should include a period of time in between each to allow the interviewer to make appropriate notes on each candidate.

8. It is important not to schedule too many interviews in one day. This can prove counterproductive.

9. The interviewer should give the candidates an opportunity to ask questions at the end of the interview.

10. It is important that the interviewer ensures that no candidate departs with the impression that their interview has been successful and that they have landed the job.

11. Candidates should be informed of the outcome of their interview as soon as possible.

The follow-up

It is crucial that follow-up action is taken quickly. Delays can mean that an organization may lose their preferred candidate to another employer during the period of time it takes to make a decision.

1. Having selected the preferred candidate, contact should be made, either by telephone or in writing, within one or two days of the interviews having taken place to make the offer of employment.
2. The offer letter (see Figure 6.3), should contain all the information that a candidate will need to allow them to make a quick decision. It is advisable to include terms and conditions of employment (see next section), and a contract of employment (see Figure 6.4). The latter should include details of the post offered, salary, working hours etc, and identify a proposed starting date.
3. It is sensible to indicate a date by when a response to the offer of employment is expected.
4. The selection process may have resulted in a second candidate whom it is felt could be offered the post if the first choice candidate decided not to take up the offer of employment. It is therefore important to keep the time-scales tight so that the second choice candidate is not lost to another employer.
5. Should your first choice candidate decide to take up the post, it is important at this stage to let other candidates know that they have been unsuccessful.

Terms and conditions of employment

It is a legal requirement to have a written statement of employment particulars. Often these terms are incorporated into a contract. A written statement of employment particulars is required to set out key areas of an employee's terms and conditions.

Every employee must receive written details of their terms and conditions of employment within two months of them starting work with an organization in order to conform to the Employment

Dear

Following your recent interview, we are pleased to offer you the post of *(insert name of post)*. Your terms and conditions of employment are as per the enclosed statement and the offer is subject to satisfactory references being received.

The following form part of your terms and conditions of employment and were discussed with you at interview.

1. You will be employed by *(name of organization)* on the organization's normal terms and conditions of employment.

2. Your salary will be £*(insert figure)* per annum, paid monthly in arrears on the last day of each month by credit transfer into your bank account.

3. Your paid annual holiday entitlement will be *(state number of days)* plus *(state number of days)* recognized public and bank holidays.

4. Your normal hours of work will be *(state number of hours per week)*, Monday to Friday. As explained at interview, it may be necessary for you to work longer hours occasionally to ensure that the responsibilities generic within the post offered are fulfilled. It is not company policy to offer additional remuneration in such cases.

5. Your employment will be subject to an initial probationary period of three months. During this period, your employment may be terminated with one week's notice on either side. On successful completion of your probationary period, your employment will be confirmed and the notice period to terminate employment will be as laid down in the enclosed terms and conditions of employment.

We very much hope that you will wish to accept our offer of employment and would ask that you telephone the undersigned to advise us of your decision. Should you accept, we can discuss and agree an acceptable commencement date. We would then require that you confirm in writing your acceptance of our offer, and at this stage we will then write to your two identified work-related referees.

I look forward to hearing from you and to welcoming you to the organization.

Yours sincerely

Name
Designation

Figure 6.3 An example of an Offer of Employment letter

Protection (Consolidation) Act 1978, as amended. Written conditions can be used to resolve disputes. It is useful to both employee and employer if the statement of terms and conditions of employment are provided when the job offer is made.

The following information must be included in all terms and conditions of employment in line with the EPCA:

- Name of the organization and the employee/potential employee.
- Job title.
- Date when employment is to begin/began.
- Indicate the date when the employee's period of continuous employment began (which might include employment with a previous employer, which would count towards their continuous employment with the organization).
- Hours of work and rate of pay.
- Holiday entitlement.
- Sickness or injury absence processes and pay.
- Pension scheme information (if one exists).
- Notice in relation to termination of employment by either side.
- Disciplinary and grievance rules and processes and the appeals procedure.

A recruitment campaign checklist

To summarize, here is a useful checklist to help the interviewer to focus and organize their recruitment campaign:

1. **Job analysis** – identify current and potential skill requirements for the post being advertised, using internal and external information (see Chapter 5).
2. **Produce:**

   a) a **job description;**
   b) a **personnel specification.**

3. **Advertise the post:**

   a) Make sure sufficient information is included to allow potential candidates to elect themselves in or out of the application process.
   b) Consider appropriate media, depending upon the type of post to be advertised:

- newspapers – local and local free newspapers, regional, national;
- specialist magazines;
- job centre;
- agencies;
- internet and internet agencies;
- careers service;
- annual milk round.

4. **Send out application pack to potential candidates** – to include job description, personnel specification and application form if this is to be used.
5. **After closing date – short-list candidates, schedule interviews and invite potential recruits** – send out any sample test materials if tests are to be a part of the selection process.
6. **Interview candidates**.
7. **Decide on successful candidate**.
8. **Send offer letter** – include: terms and conditions of employment and salary/benefits package, identify start date, venue and who should be contacted regarding a start date.
9. **Send out letters to unsuccessful candidates**. Some organizations wait until they have had confirmation of acceptance from their preferred candidate before writing to others. However, unless there is a second candidate who you would consider should your preferred choice not accept the job offer, it is good practice, and reflects well on the organization, if rejection letters are sent out promptly once decisions have been made.
10. **Induction** – ensure that the new employee is offered effective induction training to facilitate their ability to settle in quickly and perform effectively

Some tools for the selection process

Group activities

A variety of group activities can be used to aid selection. One approach may focus on the specific role and the type of individual who will fit into the team.

CONTRACT OF EMPLOYMENT

Mr/Mrs/Miss/Ms/Dr _____ Date of birth _____

(insert name in block capitals)

Address _____

_____

This agreement constitutes your written contract of employment with (insert name of organization). This offer is subject to the receipt of references that prove to be satisfactory to the organization. Your terms and conditions of employment are:

Job title:_____ Annual Salary_____

Date of joining_____ Location _____

Hours of work _____ Full/part-time _____

Details of your conditions of employment and employee benefits are included in the Employees' Handbook, a copy of which will be given to you at the start of your employment with us. A copy is also displayed on the staff Notice Board. The Employees Handbook contains details of: the Pension and Life Assurance Scheme, Holiday Entitlement, Overtime, Payments for Sickness and Accidents and Rules relating to Absence, Notice Periods, Disciplinary Rules and Procedures, Grievance and Appeals Procedures. Any future changes in terms and conditions of employment will be communicated via staff Notice Boards where these apply to all employees, or in writing to you if they relate to you personally.

Signed _____ for and on behalf of (insert company name)

I have read the above statement and have received and read a copy of the Employees' Handbook and I confirm that I understand and agree to the terms and conditions of employment detailed within these documents.

Signed _____ Date _____

N.I. No. _____ P45 enclosed (Yes/No)

Name of Bank _____

Address of Bank _____

Bank Sort Code:_____ Account No. _____

Should you require any further information or clarification of any aspects of the content of your terms and conditions of employment you should not hesitate to ask your line manager or contact (insert name of Director/Manager responsible for Human Resource matters).

Copies to: Individual Employee

Individual's Personnel File

Figure 6.4   An example of a Contract of Employment

Group activities are also used for assessing *problem-solving* ability and the individual's capacity to contribute effectively and work well as part of a team. The tasks are usually work-related. Assessment is usually by observation and it is possible to evaluate an individual's interpersonal, influencing and leadership skills during group activities.

In-tray exercises

The in-tray is usually a simulation of what a manager might find in his or her in-tray. This tends to assess an individual's ability to make appropriate decisions under pressure and within time constraints. In addition, there is an opportunity to assess whether the individual would deal appropriately with different situations and whether they realize the knock-on effect of their decisions on other employees within the organization. This approach also assesses the candidate's ability to organize and prioritize their work.

Oral presentations

A candidate is asked to develop and deliver an oral presentation. The employer may provide the topic or the candidate may be able to choose their own topic. The presentation may be flagged ahead of the interview to allow the candidate to prepare ahead and bring the presentation material with them. Alternatively, the employer may decide on the topic during the course of the selection process and give the candidate a limited time to develop a presentation on site during the overall recruitment process.

This approach assesses the candidate's verbal and non-verbal presentation skills and whether they can deliver relevant content in the time-scale allocated.

Work simulation exercises

Simulation of a typical work situation is created to assess the candidate's ability to do the job effectively. A candidate may be asked to review a company's operating statement and generate questions they would wish to ask the company's financial director. An applicant for the post of Data Input Clerk may be asked to carry out data input on a computer. This allows assessment of actual ability as opposed to an individual stating verbally how they would carry out a task.

Testing

Many large organizations have incorporated testing into their recruitment process, particularly where management recruitment is concerned. Every one of Britain's current 100 largest companies applies some kind of personality testing to its prospective employees, with 80 per cent of small to medium-sized enterprises using personality tests as part of the recruitment process.

Those who defend psychometric testing claim that they provide a reliable indication of an individual's personality and that personality is the crucial factor needed to build a successful workplace. Personality tests can indicate attitude to work, identify how conscientious and committed an individual might be, how an individual manages stress and what the individual's attitude to other people will be.

A variety of tests are available to organizations for use in the recruitment process.

Personality profiling

This usually requires the candidate to complete a personality profile document. This type of profiling can only be carried out by professionals who have been trained to analyse the results. They tend to indicate how the individual will act/react in certain situations and also give an indication of the management approach an individual might take.

Personality profiling has become almost the norm for organizations recruiting middle and senior management.

Performance tests

These use specific activities that test, for instance, keyboarding skills, flying skills etc.

Psychological tests

Psychological testing is a term that describes tools used to measure individual differences in areas such as ability and intelligence. These types of tests are most often used as an aid to selection in the recruitment process. Scoring of tests is often complex and personality profiling tests are designed to present a profile of a particular individual as previously mentioned.

Tests need to be scored by individuals who have been trained to interpret the results and in a small organization it is likely that these skills will be bought in from outside. The alternative is to train one or more individuals in the operation and scoring of psychometric testing. This may well prove not to be cost-effective if testing is not part of the normal process of the majority of recruitment for the organization.

Should the organization decide that testing should form part of the selection process, several issues need further consideration:

- Candidates should be made aware ahead of the process that testing will be used. Often, organizations send out example tests for candidates to practise ahead of the interview taking place.
- Feedback should always be given and candidates should be made aware of how they will receive this.
- All results should be made available to personnel on a 'need to know' basis only and the candidate should know who will have access to the results.
- If the purpose of testing is to assist short-listing of candidates then a variety of tests should be used. Any one test, on its own, is likely to produce a skewed picture.

Test materials are copyright to the organization that has written and produced them. Further information on testing can be obtained from the British Psychological Society (see the Useful Contacts section at the end of the book).

Assessment centres

Assessment centres can be used as an aid in the selection process. These centres use multiple methods of assessment and are operated by professionals with results being analysed by experts.

Within an assessment centre, a programme of tests, exercises and work simulations will be used. In addition, interviews will be designed to assess a wide range of abilities, skills, behavioural characteristics and potential relevance for effective performance of a specific job.

The time involved and the cost in either setting up or using an assessment centre are enormous. Whilst it can be argued that assessment centres offer a holistic assessment of the individual, the cost is prohibitive and unlikely to be an option for smaller organizations.

References

It is common practice for employers to request information regarding potential referees. Very often, current practice is to obtain references ahead of interviews taking place, but only with the candidate's permission (see Figures 6.5 and 6.6 for examples of a Reference Request letter and the Reference Request document to be completed by the referee).

References can be used to check the accuracy of details given by the applicant, for example, their job role, dates of employment etc. They are also often used to seek opinions. Referees are sometimes asked to comment generally on an individual's attributes such as honesty, cooperativeness etc.

The purpose of using a variety of selection methods is to assist in weeding out discrimination and to ensure that the most appropriate individual is appointed. However, the numbers of female managers

Dear Sir/Madam

Mr/Mrs/Ms (insert name) has applied to this company for the post of (insert name of post). We understand that he/she was employed by you for a period of (insert time-scale) between (insert dates) and that he/she was employed as (insert job title).

Mr/Mrs/Ms (insert name) has given us permission to approach you for a reference and we would be pleased if you would kindly complete the enclosed document and return it to us in the confidential stamped addressed envelope enclosed. A Job Description and Personnel Specification relating to the post applied for are enclosed for your reference

Please be assured that all information provided by you will be treated in the strictest confidence. However, we would remind you that Mr/Mrs/Ms (insert name) will have access to this document under the Data Protection Act.

We look forward to hearing from you.

Yours faithfully

Name

Designation

Figure 6.5   Example of a Reference Request letter

and individuals from ethnic minorities who are found at senior management level suggest that discrimination still occurs. In addition, age discrimination in both advertisements and the selection process are transparent. The law is set to change in 2006, with legislation being introduced to curb the use of age discrimination in the recruitment and selection process.

Most organizations seem to be looking for that elusive 'perfect' individual and whilst there is a diverse range of selection methods available to employers, by far the most popular is still the interview.

REFERENCE REQUEST

(Insert name and address of company to whom the letter and document are to be sent)

CONFIDENTIAL

Re: Mr/Mrs/Ms (insert name) – Reference

I confirm that the above named individual was employed by this organization from _____ to _____ and that their Job Title was _____.

My comments regarding the suitability of Mr/Mrs/Ms (insert name) to carry out the duties identified in the job description provided are:

Regarding the personal attributes included in the Personnel Specification, I would comment as follows:

If you would like to add any further information, please do so here:

Signed:

Designation:

Company Stamp:

Date:

Figure 6.6   Example of a Reference Request document to be completed by the referee

RECRUITMENT AGENCIES

Some large organizations use recruitment agencies as part of their selection process. Agencies can be expensive, with typical fees ranging from between 15 per cent and 25 per cent of the new employee's annual salary. A good agency will usually advertise the post and short-list and meet candidates before recommending them to an organization. All these services are usually included in the one-off fee. Most agencies have a large database of potential employees and so they can be an efficient way of getting a new employee quickly.

It is crucial that an organization fully briefs an agency of its requirements and that feedback is provided to the agency on candidates that the organization has interviewed but who have proved to be unsuitable.

Organizations should consider using more than one agency and there should be some agreement regarding claw-back of partial fees if the individual leaves within a specified period of time, say, within one or two months, for instance.

Agencies vary widely and there are good and bad operators. This applies equally to those agencies operating on the internet.

INTERNET RECRUITMENT

The growth in the use of the internet for recruitment purposes has been significant in the past few years. Over 85 per cent of companies are now using the internet to handle enquiries for jobs and applications, and more than 70 per cent are attracting candidates from information displayed on company websites.

Advantages of using the internet for recruitment purposes are:

- The time saved in the recruitment cycle.
- The potential to draw applicants from a wider field.
- Information is available 24 hours a day, seven days a week worldwide.
- Organizations portray an up-to-date image and approach.

Disadvantages include:

- The internet would not be the first point of contact for every person seeking a job.

■ The internet makes the application process easier and there is potential for organizations to be swamped with applications.

Organizations usually include an e-mail address so that potential applicants can request an application pack, or other relevant documentation, more immediately from the website. Organizations may also allow applications by e-mail. Electronically received information can be circulated quickly to interested managers within the organization via a secure computer network.

Computerized selection software

Computer software is also now available that can aid the selection process. This software tends to look for specific words and phrases and is a quick and simple method of short-listing applications received electronically.

However, it is possible that potentially strong candidates could be missed using electronic selection processes. An individual who would otherwise be considered strong may not use the words and phrases being sought by the selection software and would therefore be rejected. Companies need to consider carefully whether this approach to selection is appropriate for their organization.

Task

Review your organization's current recruitment campaign process:

1. How closely does it match that detailed in the recruitment campaign checklist detailed earlier in this chapter?
2. What are the differences?
3. How could your organization's recruitment process be improved?
4. Would you propose different processes for different levels of post, ie, manager, clerical, production line etc?

Task

Does your company currently have an Equal Opportunities Policy?

1. If it does, review the content in line with the policy statement featured earlier in this chapter. How could your policy be improved?
2. If your organization does not currently have an Equal Opportunities Policy, analyse your current operational procedures and produce a draft Equal Opportunities Policy document to be discussed, revised and implemented as soon as possible.

Case study: Delicious Yoghurts Ltd

You are the Personnel Manager of Delicious Yoghurts Ltd. In view of the continuing expansion of the business, it has been decided that the organization needs to recruit a Sales Manager to help to support and develop the sales team.

The person recruited will need to be an effective people manager and have business development experience as well as project management skills. In addition, he/she should understand performance-related pay and be able to motivate a sales team whose major proportion of income depends on sales performance against targets.

Task

Identify the selection process you would propose to ensure that you are able to recruit the right individual to the post of Sales Manager for Delicious Yoghurts Ltd.

Case study: Organic Juice Co Ltd

You are responsible for recruitment of all production personnel at the main depot of the Organic Juice Co Ltd and you need to recruit five additional workers for the company's packing line due to a sudden upturn in business.

All the employees who work in the packing department are female, including the Supervisor. You pay 50p per hour above the current minimum hourly rate laid down by the government.

Task

1. Identify where it would be most appropriate to advertise these posts for the Organic Juice case study to ensure that you are successful in recruiting the required numbers quickly.
2. What will the application process be?

Case study: The Luscious Sandwich Catering Corp

You are responsible for recruitment at The Luscious Sandwich Catering Corp. The organization has grown significantly during the past few months, and as a result, the Managing Director has become more and more involved in the marketing side of the business.

It has been decided that the organization would benefit from employing a Financial Manager who will also take responsibility for administration activities within the organization.

Task

Produce a proposal document for discussion with the Managing Director of The Luscious Sandwich Catering Corp regarding your suggestions for an appropriate recruitment and selection process. Remember to consider and include the following:

- Produce a job description and personnel specification for the role of Financial Manager. What are the main tasks for this job role, and what are the main personal attributes you expect to find within the individual who will eventually fill this post?
- Using the job description and personnel specification you have generated, develop an advertisement and identify and cost appropriate media.
- Identify the selection methods you would propose to use.
- Who will be involved in the recruitment process and what will their role(s) be?
- Develop documentation that will support the personnel involved in the recruitment process and that will best inform the selection decision.

Case study: Disability Discrimination Act (DDA)

The Disability Discrimination Act 2004 compels employers to make reasonable adjustments to their premises where a physical feature may make it difficult for disabled people to make use of their services. The alternative is to provide those services by some other means.

The phrase 'reasonable adjustments' can be interpreted in many different ways and changes that are likely to take place will depend on many considerations, some of which will depend upon company resources and constraints imposed by local planning restrictions.

The Act expects that common sense will prevail and that organizations will ensure that where reasonable, access to company services and premises are made available to the disabled.

Task

1. How accessible are your premises to candidates who attend for interview who may have a physical disability and/or may be wheelchair users?
2. What, if any, changes to recruitment processes would you need to make to ensure that physically disabled candidates are afforded equal opportunity to access your premises and be able to take part in recruitment activities?

7

Performance appraisal

All managers appraise their staff on an informal basis daily. The annual appraisal interview is the formal process that allows managers to assess the performance of an individual. The process should also ensure that fairness and objectivity are inherent within the judgements made.

The purpose of a staff appraisal system is generally to help improve the efficiency and effectiveness of both the individual and ultimately, the organization. An appraisal interview provides the opportunity to review employee performance and assess whether there is potential for improvement within each individual. Appraisals can be used for a number of purposes, including:

- *A performance review* – which is an opportunity to assess an individual's level of performance throughout the year and also to be able to identify whether any development/training is required to assist them in improving their skills and knowledge base.
- *A reward review* – this relates directly to whether an individual has achieved, or even beaten, the required performance level and therefore is entitled to a bonus or pay increase.

It is difficult to expect an individual to assess their own performance effectively and realistically and to be able to identify training and development needs if the outcome would disadvantage them financially. Therefore, there is an argument that suggests that performance appraisal should not be linked to pay.

OBJECTIVES OF APPRAISAL

The overall objectives of appraisal are to improve the performance of individuals, which should ultimately result in improved organizational performance. The main objectives of appraisal are to:

- identify the strengths and weaknesses of each employee, based on past performance;
- provide an opportunity to identify areas for further development and improvement;
- identify the training and development needs of each individual;
- set realistic and achievable targets and goals for the future;
- try to assess an individual's future potential for possible development and promotion;
- assist in career planning and development for the individual;
- identify levels of bonus or salary increase if the appraisal process is to be used for this purpose.

The appraisal process should be systematic. It should be taken seriously by all who are involved, and the system should address the following problems:

- Specific criteria should be identified, against which performance can be measured.
- There should be a standard framework for recording the outcome of the appraisal interview, which allows the manager to identify and record important issues, whilst at the same time, keeping paperwork to a minimum.
- Time must be allocated to allow both the appraiser and the appraisee to contribute to the process effectively.

Assessing potential

Assessing potential is useful in identifying those personnel who are suitable for promotion and also in deciding how the individual's abilities can be best employed for the benefit of both the organization and the individual.

Assessing general potential assists in identifying the type and levels of work an employee might have the potential to perform. This type of assessment would be based on personnel and training records and performance reviews.

Goal setting

When performance targets are handled appropriately they tend to motivate the individual. Therefore, the objectives of any appraisal process should be SMART, ie:

Specific (not generalized or vague)
Measurable (performance is measured objectively)
Agreed (by both parties and not imposed)
Realistic (able to be achieved)
Time-constrained (to achieve specific targets within a set time-scale).

APPRAISAL PROCEDURES

An organization needs to consider the following issues if it is to develop a fair and effective appraisal procedure:

- There is a need to identify specific criteria for assessment. This could be based on a job analysis exercise, personnel specification, job description, identified performance standards etc.
- There should be an opportunity for both the manager and the appraisee to produce a brief report on the individual's performance.
- An appraisal interview should provide the opportunity for an honest exchange of views in terms of the individual's performance against targets, identification of areas for improvement, opportunities for training and further development, etc.

- An action plan should be produced as a direct result of the appraisal interview, which identifies how, and by when, improvements and/or targets are to be achieved by the individual concerned.
- Ongoing reviews should be carried out to monitor the progress of the individual employee towards achieving the agreed target(s).

A range of approaches to identify appropriate criteria can be adopted. These vary from those that are non-specific and based solely on a manager's judgement, to those that incorporate aspects of psychology and consider behaviour as part of the process. It must be highlighted here that a manager's judgement can be very subjective and this can undermine the process.

A more objective approach would be to introduce a results-orientated scheme, based on the principles of management by objectives. This approach would provide an opportunity to review an individual's performance against specified targets and would be wholly results-orientated. The targets would have been agreed in advance by both the individual and their manager together. The advantages of this approach are:

- The individual is more involved in appraising their own performance because of the opportunity offered to evaluate success or progress in achieving jointly agreed targets.
- The manager takes on a problem-solving role to identify what is required to assist the individual to improve their performance.

If such a scheme is to be successful, the targets to be set will need to be carefully considered. There is little point in setting unachievable targets, as this will prove to be a demotivator for the individual. It will also be important to evaluate not only success or failure against targets, but also the reasons for failure, and equally, any opportunities that arise from success.

If a results-orientated approach is to be adopted and be successful, it will be necessary for the organization to consider the following for each of its employees:

1. What are the aims of the job?
2. What are the key outcomes that will result in the achievement of the job aims, and what are the key tasks involved in achieving them?
3. Performance standards must be agreed for the key tasks.
4. Short-term goals must be identified and action plans produced to assist in review and achievement of targets.
5. Effective monitoring and control is crucial.

Management training

Whether the appraisal system is a new initiative or the system is a proposed revision of a current process, managers will need to be trained to ensure that they are proficient in carrying out effective appraisal interviewing and assessing an individual's performance within the context of the overall appraisal process.

Communication and commitment

It is crucial that prior to the introduction of an appraisal process, its nature and purpose should be made clear. There should be commitment from the top level of management within the organization, and appraisal should be directly related to the achievement of corporate objectives. Any system should be amended regularly to ensure that the process is carried out properly and there should be an appeals procedure, which is available for use in exceptional circumstances. The appraisal process is detailed in the next section.

The appraisal process

It is advisable to develop documentation that will facilitate the appraisal process. The documentation does not have to be particularly sophisticated but it does have to provide the opportunity for both sides to be able to reflect on, and evaluate, an individual's performance.

Specially designed forms will ensure that there is a consistent approach to the appraisal process company-wide:

1. The manager and the appraisee should each have a document, which should be completed prior to the appraisal interview taking place.
2. These forms are then exchanged, either at the interview, or prior to it, and will form the basis for the discussion. These give a focus to the appraisal interview and offer the opportunity to prepare ahead.
3. The form should be designed so that each section is explained clearly, and there may be a set of guidelines to ensure that all parties are clear on what is required.
4. The criteria used to assess performance should be objective and not subjective. It is appropriate that these should concentrate on areas of performance that could be improved. However, it is also important to ensure that good performance during the previous period is highlighted, acknowledged and praised.
5. There should be a separate form, which is completed by the appraiser (usually the line manager of the appraisee), which reflects the agreed outcome of the appraisal. Both the appraiser and the appraisee should sign the completed form.
6. There should also be an opportunity for the individual to be able to appeal against either elements of, or all of the content of the appraisal document and the procedure to be followed should form part of the appraisal process documentation. However, instances where there is a need to instigate the appeals process should be rare.
7. The guidelines should clearly identify what should be done with the appraisal forms, ie, will they be stored in the individual's personnel file? Who will be responsible for ensuring that relevant actions are carried out? Will the line manager keep a copy of the completed appraisal documents?
8. The design of the process will depend upon what approach to appraisal is to be adopted by the organization.

An example of a Staff Appraisal Scheme, together with a set of relevant documents, appear in Figures 7.1 to 7.7 at the end of this chapter.

PRINCIPLES OF PERFORMANCE APPRAISAL

Individuals who are involved in setting their own targets will be clear on what they are expected to achieve. It is crucial that specific, relevant feedback is given relating to their overall performance. This should also relate to their performance against the targets as agreed and set during the last appraisal round.

Principles upon which appraisal should be based include the following:

1. Sufficient relevant information should be available so that objective judgements can be made.
2. The completed documentation should accurately reflect the verbal interchange that took place during the appraisal interview.

There has been a shift during recent years that has led to the introduction of terms and conditions of employment that apply to all levels of employees within an organization. There has also been an increase in the introduction of flexible working practices to facilitate the changing needs of business and to ensure that organizations can be more dynamic in responding to customer needs. Because of these changes, it is now possible to appraise every member of the workforce, not just management and clerical staff.

As mentioned previously, it is usual for an individual's line manager to carry out the appraisal. However, this may not be possible if the manager has a wide span of control. The time needed to appraise all members of his/her staff would be impractical. In such instances, an organization would need to delegate the appraiser role to supervisors and/or other relevant managers to facilitate an effective process.

The frequency with which appraisal is carried out should directly relate to the nature of the organization. In a dynamic environment where there is constant ongoing change, appraisal is likely to be more frequent.

A system of open reporting, where all aspects of the process are transparent is more likely to result in agreement and in the counter-signing of the agreed outcome.

OTHER FORMS OF APPRAISAL

Peer appraisal

Some appraisal processes include an element where individuals are appraised by their peers. In other instances, individuals may appraise themselves; however, this approach is more usually found as one element of the process of all successful and effective appraisal systems.

Upward appraisal

Upward appraisal is a process that involves both the appraisee's subordinates and their manager in the appraisal of their performance. There are certain advantages to the organization where this approach to appraisal is adopted. Subordinates are familiar with their line managers and are able to identify strengths and weaknesses. A rating system tends to be used where individuals rate their manager's performance, say on a scale of 1 to 5 where 1 is excellent and 5 is unacceptable.

The drawbacks involved in this approach are that subordinates may fear that they will be victimized by their manager if their feedback is less than positive. In addition, it is likely that some managers will ignore negative feedback and take no action to improve their performance.

360-degree appraisal

There are increasing instances of 360-degree appraisal feedback. This involves feedback being sought from a variety of groups within the working environment. In such instances, an individual's performance could be assessed by their line manager, their subordinates, their peers, and by themselves, as well as by both internal and external customers.

APPRAISAL AS A MOTIVATOR

Identifying challenging but achievable goals for improvement of performance helps individuals to clarify goals and set a value in terms of any associated monetary reward.

Constructive feedback on performance tends to be a motivator, even where the feedback is negative. Feedback allows the individual to assess what they need to do to improve their performance and helps to motivate them to accomplish greater levels of achievement.

People sometimes react poorly to criticism. Some individuals find ways of explaining away their poor performance. Getting the level of criticism right takes skill, and managers should be aware that criticism of an individual who has low self-esteem could be damaging.

An appraisee often finds the appraisal interview stressful. The expectation is of a positive experience, which sometimes is not the case.

PROBLEMS WITH APPRAISAL

An individual may become defensive if they perceive the appraisal process to be a threat. This is usually the case when the outcome of the appraisal is seen as a threat to the promotional prospects of the individual, or where the individual subsequently suffers financial loss where the appraisal process is linked to pay.

There are also those managers who feel uncomfortable making judgements that affect an employee's future. The appraiser may be biased, either in favour of, or against, a particular individual. Whether this is conscious or unconscious bias is irrelevant because either way, this will affect the overall outcome of the appraisal. Processes that do not have specified criteria will usually result in the appraiser making subjective and improper judgements about the individual.

Time can also be an issue. For the appraisal process to be effective, both the appraiser and the appraisee will need to be able to allocate adequate time to deal with the process effectively.

An individual's experience within an organization may suggest that the appraisal process is a waste of time, has no relevance to the job and no ongoing follow-up action. In other words, it is perceived as a paper exercise with no benefits to either the individual or the organization.

The organization culture may be such that appraisal is not taken seriously. Interviewers may be untrained and not given adequate time to prepare and the appraisee may not be encouraged to contribute.

Task

1. Does your organization currently operate an appraisal system? If 'Yes', evaluate its effectiveness in achieving the organization's objectives.
2. Does the system need to be revised? If so, what actions will need to be taken?

Task

Your organization does not currently operate an appraisal system:

1. Identify what specific steps you will need to take to introduce an appropriate and relevant appraisal system.
2. How would you propose to communicate the aims and objectives of the new appraisal system to employees to ensure that its introduction is successful and valued by employees?

APPRAISAL-RELATED PAY

Appraisal-related pay is a method of payment where an individual's pay package is based on regular assessments of how they perform their job.

Performance-related appraisal is often linked to a scheme that results in additional payments being made over and above the normal pay scale and is based on recognition for strong performance. This approach can be used to replace all, or part of general pay increases. Introducing appraisal-related pay involves a significant shift in organizational culture. This is often introduced at senior management level initially before being considered for a wider roll out.

Many different types and sizes of organization have introduced appraisal-related pay, but it is more often found in larger organizations. Senior management will need to decide whether the introduction of ARP is relevant for their organization. Additional issues to consider would be:

- Is the current pay system fair and does it allow the organization to recruit and retain employees?
- Does the current system motivate employees and encourage productivity?
- Does the system measure performance and is it controllable?

In order to compete more effectively in the marketplace, some organizations have found that employees can be encouraged to improve productivity by paying for higher performance based on measurable criteria. This allows effective targeting of resources and assists in retaining high performing employees. Some of the benefits include improved quality of product and/or service. Some employees will be pleased that high performance is recognized and this can improve morale.

However, if the system is designed and introduced inappropriately, there will be a negative impact on employee relations. If communication of what is required to achieve higher pay is not understood and an open system of management is not apparent, and if employees are unable to see that rules are applied consistently, then this will act as a demotivator. The scheme would need to be carefully developed to ensure that its introduction was smooth and accepted by all employees.

IMPROVING THE PROCESS

All appraisal systems should be assessed periodically to check for:

- *Relevance* – does the process have a purpose and is this clearly expressed? Are the criteria relevant?
- *Fairness* – is the process objectively operated?
- *Intent* – is there management commitment to the system, and are interviewers properly trained? Is enough time allocated to ensure the process is operated effectively and is there a perceivable link between performance and reward?
- *Cooperation* – is the process participative and is the appraisee given time to adequately prepare? Are appraisals held regularly and do specific conclusions and plans result?
- *Efficiency* – is the process costly and difficult to administer and is the process too time-consuming?

If the organization is to be able to identify relevant opportunities that may be available to the individual in the future, and feed this back to them, then the opportunity to review potential becomes crucial. It is important that there is a formal process in situ to be able to assess, at regular intervals, an individual's progress in terms of skills and career development. This helps to facilitate succession planning and identify skill gaps within the organization.

Task

You are one of a number of managers who will be appraising staff during the imminent round of appraisal interviews within your organization.

1. Identify an appropriate location. Preferably, the interviews should take place on neutral ground, and not in your own office.

2. What do you need to do to prepare ahead?
3. What documentation will you use?

Scenario – the hotel industry
It has been suggested that human resources top the list of problems that will face the hotel industry in the future. Organizations will need to invest in recruitment, training and improved reward packages if they are to be able to recruit and retain quality staff in the future.

Task

As a Human Resource Adviser, consider whether an effective appraisal process would assist those hotel and catering businesses in the scenario above that are finding recruitment and retention of staff difficult.

1. If 'Yes' identify specifically what impact you feel such a process would have on the recruitment and retention of personnel.
2. If 'No' what ideas can you put forward that might overcome the projected difficulties?

Case study: The Excellent Food Company Limited

The Excellent Food Company Limited employs several thousand staff on a nationwide basis. The company operates a large chain of small retail outlets together with a fleet of mobile vans. The company aims to service those geographically widespread communities that have suffered from the closure of so many small businesses during the past few years. Its size and buying power has allowed the company to grow its business successfully across a seven-year period.

Appraisals are currently applied to management, clerical staff and sales personnel only and take place annually in February. The current appraisal process has been used for the past four years but has had minor changes made to it each year to reflect the changing focus of the business.

Targets for performance are set annually by the management board and these are communicated initially to the two Operations Managers, then to Regional Managers who decide upon and communicate individual targets to Area Representatives and Van Sales personnel. These targets are not discussed with the individual beforehand.

Whilst Area Representatives and Van Sales personnel are expected to achieve their individual targets, the regions are judged, not on individual performance but on the performance of each regional area as a whole.

Whilst the company is solid and performing well, it has been going through a process of re-engineering and re-structuring to make the operation more efficient and effective. This is being done in order to increase the level of net profit available for dividend distribution to its shareholders.

The current appraisal system is seen as a purely paper exercise by the majority of the Area Representatives and Van Sales personnel. However, individuals are reluctant to voice their opinions in case they find their name on the list of those included in the next round of redundancies.

In addition, in September, the Operations Manager for the North and Midlands has told his Regional Managers that those individuals who do not achieve at least 60 per cent of their target for the latest product promotion will fail their appraisal.

After the last round of appraisals, held earlier in the year, the appraisal scores of all Area Representatives and Van Sales personnel were downgraded to fall in line with a projected performance level, which had been calculated using a formula based on actual results. The argument was that if the levels of appraisal scores were correct, then the company should have been performing much more profitably than is currently the case. Despite the negative impact this action had on the morale of all personnel affected by this change, there was no right of appeal.

Task

You are the newly appointed Human Resource Manager for The Excellent Food Company Limited in the case study above.

1. Having reviewed the content of this chapter, what issues can you identify that need to be addressed?
2. Prepare a paper that you would present to the Board of Directors, which details your concerns; your suggestions for improvement; the benefits to the organization should your ideas be adopted.

STAFF APPRAISAL SCHEME

1. **Purpose and Scope**

1.1   This scheme applies to all full-time and part-time members of staff.

1.2   The scheme is based on the belief that all members of staff have a right to:

- a clear understanding of their department's expectations of them;
- an opportunity to have a detailed discussion of their contribution to the achievement of departmental and company goals; and
- to feel valued as an individual.

Staff appraisal is designed to facilitate effective two-way communication and is the mechanism for identifying training and development needs linked to company objectives.

1.3   This scheme is not linked to procedures that determine pay.

2. **Timing and Frequency of Appraisal**

2.1   All staff will be appraised on an annual basis. All Appraisals will take place during the month of March each year.

3. **Appraisers**

3.1   All staff will be reviewed by their line manager.

3.2   The department manager will decide which staff will undertake the role of Appraiser. No manager should appraise more than 10 members of staff. The department manager will nominate alternative Appraisers as required. The department manager should see all complete Appraisal forms for staff in their department whether they are the Appraiser or not.

3.3   All Appraisers should have completed appropriate training before being asked to carry out Appraisal interviews. The Personnel and Training Manager will keep a record of all staff who are trained to carry out Appraisal interviews and will also arrange training where required.

4. **The Appraisal Process**

4.1   The Appraisal process proves to be most beneficial when the following conditions are met:

- there is an open and honest joint review of past achievements;
- future goals are identified;
- assistance and support is offered to ensure the achievement of identified goals;
- both and Appraiser and Appraisee prepare thoroughly ahead of the Appraisal interview taking place;

Figure 7.1   An example of a Staff Appraisal Scheme

STAFF APPRAISAL SCHEME (continued)

□ sufficient time is allocated for the meeting;

□ a suitable room is available, which is private and will ensure freedom from interruptions.

5.   Preparation

5.1   Prior to the Appraisal process taking place, Heads of Department should ensure that all Appraisers have been trained and are aware of both departmental and company aims, objectives and priorities for the period of time under review.

5.2   Part A of the Appraisal documentation is designed to facilitate preparation for the Appraisal meeting. This should be completed by the Appraisee and submitted to the Appraiser one week before the Appraisal meeting is to take place. Appraisees should consider key tasks that they have undertaken successfully since their last appraisal. In addition, strengths should be noted and new skills identified that might be needed in relation to aims and objectives for the coming 12 months. Consideration should be given to the support and training/development provided by their manager and/or colleagues and whether this has helped them to carry out their duties effectively. Appraisees should also try to identify any general issues they wish to discuss that they feel might lead to greater efficiency and effectiveness.

5.3   Part A of the Appraisal document should be accompanied by a current job description and any information regarding significant changes in the individual's CV that have occurred since the last Appraisal took place.

5.4   Prior to the Appraisal interview, the Appraiser should read Part A of the Appraisal document and any accompanying paperwork. The Appraiser should also consider the individual's achievements and contribution to the work of the department, their strengths and any new skills that they might need to assist in achieving their future objectives.

6.   Appraisal interview

6.1   The Appraisal interview should include a discussion of any changes to the individual's job during the past 12 months and/or any foreseen changes in the future. A review of workloads and working arrangements should also be undertaken. The interview should also explore working practices that have affected the work and effectiveness of the Appraisee whether these are departmental or company-wide. The career aspirations of the Appraisee should also facilitate the discussion.

Figure 7.1   continued

STAFF APPRAISAL SCHEME (continued)

6.2   The Appraisal interview should centre on the work of the Appraisee in the light of his/her major responsibilities during the period under review. Progress made against objectives set at the last Appraisal should be examined. If objectives have changed or have not been met, reasons for this should be examined. Objectives for the forthcoming Appraisal period should be discussed and agreed.

6.3   It is important to close the meeting with both parties having a mutual understanding of what needs to be done and what action is to be taken, by whom and any follow-up actions necessary.

7.   Documentation

7.1   Part B of the Appraisal document should be completed within five working days of the meeting and should summarize the main points discussed and record the objectives that have been agreed. Any action needed by the line manager and/or others to facilitate successful achievement of the objectives should be noted. Both Appraiser and Appraisee should sign the record of the Appraisal meeting and each should retain a copy.

7.2   Part C of the Appraisal document should be completed by the Appraiser and this should record any training and/or development needs agreed during the Appraisal meeting. The document should be signed by the Appraisee, the Appraiser and the Personnel and Training Manager. Staff wishing to request financial assistance for part-time study for relevant vocation and/or professional qualifications should identify their intentions in the course of discussion during the Appraisal interview.

7.3   The Appraisal interview form is confidential and will be kept in the individual's Personnel file. The form will be accessible to the Appraiser, the Appraisee, the Head of Department and the Personnel and Training Manager.

8.   Follow-up

8.1   It is essential that follow-up action identified during the Appraisal meeting be carried out. Appraisers should meet informally with Appraisees through the year to discuss progress against objectives and the outcome of any training and development undertaken.

8.2   The Head of Department should agree the priority of the different training needs identified.

Figure 7.1   continued

STAFF APPRAISAL SCHEME (continued)

8.3   In the event of a disagreement regarding the content of part B or C of the Appraisal documentation, which cannot be resolved by the Appraisee and Appraiser, the Appraisee should raise their concerns with the Appraiser's line manager within five working days of receipt of the completed Appraisal document. The attached form should be used for this purpose. The Appraiser's line manager and the Personnel and Training Manager will meet with the Appraiser and Appraisee to consider the concerns raised and will then advise the Appraisee of the decision in writing within 10 working days of the meeting taking place.

9.   Monitoring the Policy

9.1   Heads of Department are responsible for ensuring that the policy is implemented and the Personnel and Training Manager will monitor the completion of staff Appraisal.

Figure 7.1   continued

STAFF APPRAISAL SCHEME

When completed, copies of all sections of this form, except Part C, should be stored in the individual's confidential personnel file.

Name of Appraisee _____

Current Post _____

Department _____

Date of appointment to present post_____

Name of Appraiser _____

Date of Meeting _____

NB A job description or list of responsibilities together with a summary of any significant changes to your CV since your last Appraisal should be attached to Part A of the form.

PART A

To be completed by the individual Appraisee and passed to the Appraiser at least five working days prior to the date of the Appraisal meeting.

1. A summary of your main achievements in relation to the aims and objectives for the Appraisal period under review. Identify any significant changes in your responsibilities since the last Appraisal.

2. A summary of any factors that have affected achievement of your aims and objectives and/or your contribution to the work of the department over the Appraisal period.

3. Major activities, tasks and priorities, which you anticipate in the coming Appraisal period and any training and/or support you will need to assist you in achieving these.

PART B

A summary of the interview. To be completed by the Appraiser after the Appraisal meeting has taken place.

1. Identify significant achievements since the last Appraisal took place.

2. Identify any aims and objectives not achieved and any factors that have affected non-achievement. Where relevant, identify actions agreed to reduce the impact of such factors in the future.

3. Objectives should be agreed for the coming Appraisal period. These should address all main elements of the Appraisee's responsibilities.

Figure 7.2 Staff Appraisal Scheme – instructions to staff

STAFF APPRAISAL SCHEME (continued)

4.   Identify any actions required within the Department or elsewhere within the organization to enable aims and objectives to be achieved.

Signed: (Appraiser)

Date:

PART C

After completion by the Appraiser, both the Appraiser and the Appraisee should retain a copy of Part C and the original should be sent to the Personnel and Training Manager.

During the course of the Appraisal meeting the following areas of training and/or development need to have been identified. Please be as specific as possible.

Description of training and/or development needed:

Target date:

Summary and evaluation of training and/or development undertaken since the last Appraisal (if none please make that clear):

1.   To be signed by the following:

Appraisee's signature:

Appraisee's name:

Department:

Appraiser's signature:

Appraiser's name:

Department:

Date of Appraisal meeting:

Head of Department:

Date:

Figure 7.2   continued

STAFF APPRAISAL SCHEME

NOTE:　　　When complete, all sections of this form should be stored securely.

Name of Appraisee: _____

Post held: _____

Date of appointment: _____

Department: _____

Name of Appraiser: _____

Date of meeting: _____

Figure 7.3　Cover sheet for Staff Appraisal Scheme

PART A

To be completed by the Appraisee and passed to the Appraiser at least five working days prior to the Appraisal meeting.

1.   Summarize your main achievements based on your aims and objectives

for the period under review. Include any significant changes in your

responsibilities since your last Appraisal.

2.   Summarize any factors that have affected you achieving your aims and

objectives.

3.   Identify major activities, tasks and priorities, which you anticipate

during the next 12 months. Identify any training and development that

you will need to assist you in achieving them.

Figure 7.4   Part A of the Appraisal documentation

PART B

Summary of discussion. To be completed by the Appraiser following the meeting.

1. Significant achievements since the last review.

2. Aims and objectives not achieved. Any factors that have affected achievement of objectives and, if relevant, any actions agreed to reduce the impact of such factors in the future.

3. Aims and objectives agreed for the next 12-month period, which should relate directly to the Appraisee's main responsibilities.

Figure 7.5   Part B of the Appraisal documentation

PART B (continued)

4.   Any action required within the department/company-wide to facilitate

achievement of the objectives.

Signed:

(Appraiser)

Date:

I have read the comments made by the Appraiser and have nothing to

add/wish to add: **(to be completed by the Appraisee)**

Signed:

(Appraisee)

Date:

Figure 7.5   continued

PART C

After completion by the Appraiser, both the Appraiser and the Appraisee should retain a copy of Part C. The original should be stored in the employee's confidential Personnel file.

On completion of the Appraisal process, this page to be forwarded to the Personnel and Training Manager.

During the course of the Appraisal meeting, the following training/development needs have been identified.

NB Include any training identified to improve performance in the current role. In addition, include any development needs that will equip the Appraisee to undertake a wider and/or different/more senior role.

Description of training and development needed. (Please be as specific as possible.)

Target date

Figure 7.6 Part C of the Appraisal documentation

PART C (continued)

Summary and evaluation of training undertaken during the last 12-month period. (If none please state 'none'.)

1. To be signed by the following:

Appraisee's signature:
Appraisee's name (in caps):
Department:

Appraiser's signature:
Appraiser's name (in caps):
Department:
Date of Appraisal meeting:

Figure 7.6   continued

STAFF APPRAISAL APPEAL

Form to be used in the event of a disagreement between the Appraiser and

Appraisee regarding the content of a completed Staff Appraisal Form.

Appraisee's name:_____ **Department:** _____

Appraiser's name: _____ **Designation:** _____

Please specify your areas of concern regarding the completed Staff Appraisal

document.

Appraisee's signature:_____ **Date:**_____

I note that the above Appraisee wishes to raise concerns regarding his/her

Staff Appraisal.

Appraiser's signature: _____ **Date:**_____

Once this form is completed and signed it should be forwarded to the

Appraiser's line manager together with a copy of parts A, B and C. The Personnel

and Training Manager and the Appraiser's line manager will meet with both

parties to hear and consider the Appraisee's concerns. The Appraisee will be

informed within 10 working days of the outcome of their appeal.

Figure 7.7 Staff Appraisal Scheme Appeal document

8

Attendance and absence management

ATTENDANCE MANAGEMENT

Attendance management is becoming a major issue for many organizations that are finding the levels of staff absence unacceptable. The importance of managing absence effectively, particularly short-term absence, is proving to be a crucial aspect of effective people management. Recent reports have identified that the amount of downtime lost across the United Kingdom because of employees taking off sick days, or 'sickies' as they have become known, is currently costing organizations a massive £11 billion per annum. This equates to 176 million days lost in 2003, 10 million more than in 2002 and is an average of 7.2 days per employee.

In addition to cost, the disruption to manufacturing industries and service sector organizations is having a major impact on the quality of products and customer service offered. The overall loss of business is difficult to assess but the impact is likely to result in the loss of customers and, in some cases, possibly even closure of a business, with the resulting loss of jobs.

There is a need to encourage employees to attend work as opposed to taking time off. A large proportion of employers now use 'triggers' and 'return-to-work' interviews to help control what is proving to be a growing problem. These particular mechanisms assist in tightening control and are designed to encourage individuals to attend work as opposed to taking time off. Triggers help to identify cases that need further investigation, and return-to-work interviews take place following a period of absence.

Task

1. Does your organization have a system that assists you in monitoring personnel absence? If 'Yes', is it effective?
2. If 'No', why not?
3. Identify how you might improve the current process or introduce a process to help your organization to better manage absence.
4. How will you communicate the changes and/or introduction of the system to all employees?

ABSENCE INVESTIGATION

If the company intends to set up control systems that are effective, it must first of all identify exactly what is meant by the term 'absenteeism'. A decision will need to be made on how absence is to be measured, and it will be necessary to understand the main causes of absence.

■ An organization must first assess:

- how widespread or significant the absence problem is;
- the level of both direct and indirect costs that are associated with absence;
- how much time is lost through absence.

■ It is important to identify whether there are specific areas within the organization where absence is greater. If there are departments and/or groups that have particularly high absence levels, these should be identified. At the same time, the level of individual absence should be established.

▓ What are the causes of absence?

- Are these job-related?
- Would an analysis of the design of work be useful?
- Is there a problem with, say, the supervisor or manager?

▓ If the organization has absence controls, it is essential to ensure that these are relevant to the causes of absence identified. It is important to establish whether the current systems are effective.

▓ Any process that purports to assist in reducing and controlling absence levels must take into account the nature of the organization, its culture as well as location and cost. Introducing an inappropriate system will result in the inability of the organization to monitor and control the process as well as non-achievement of objectives.

▓ Before introducing any absence control process, it is crucial that the changes are explained to all personnel. In addition, management should try to identify ahead, strategies for overcoming possible objections/responses.

▓ Any new process needs to be monitored to assess its effectiveness; therefore criteria should be identified that allows the system to be assessed and any benefits identified.

An example of a Sickness Absence Policy Statement is detailed in Figure 8.1.

Most absence falls into two categories:

1. *Authorized absence*, which relates to absence for a genuine reason such as illness, absence on compassionate grounds etc. Figure 8.2 is an example of an Individual Absence Request Form, which could be used in instances where an individual knows ahead when they will need to be absent – for instance, in the case of annual leave, a hospital appointment, jury service etc.
2. *Unauthorized absence* relates to instances of absence where it is difficult to ascertain whether the individual had a legitimate reason for being away from work.

SICKNESS ABSENCE POLICY STATEMENT

1.   Scope and Purpose of Policy

1.1   This policy relates to all staff and establishes guidelines for managers and staff relating to sickness absence. The intention is to enable sickness absence to be dealt with consistently and fairly across the organization. Included are procedures for reporting and recording sickness absence.

1.2   Staff who are ill will be treated sympathetically and every effort will be made to assist recovery and safeguard employment. However, the loss of working days through repeated sickness absence can be costly to the organization. Absence through sickness also puts additional pressure on colleagues.

1.3   Details of sick pay entitlement are included in the employee's terms and conditions of employment, which form part of every employee's contract of employment.

2.   Reporting and Recording Procedures

2.1   If a member of staff becomes ill at work, his/her line manager should give permission for the individual to leave work and to seek medical advice where appropriate. Absence relating to appointments with a doctor, dentist, hospital or cancer screening, are to be treated as legitimate reasons for absence.

2.2   A member of staff who is sick and cannot attend work should contact his/her line manager within 30 minutes of the time when s/he normally starts work. Staff should make contact personally and not rely on others to do this on their behalf.

2.3   If a member of staff believes that his/her condition relates to an activity or incident at work, s/he should inform his/her line manager. An Accident Report form will need to be completed and passed to the Company's Health and Safety Officer.

2.4   Department Managers are responsible for ensuring that a record is kept of the whereabouts of all staff in their department, eg, sick leave, holidays, staff working off site. Department Managers are responsible for ensuring that all sickness absence is recorded. When reporting absence from work due to sickness, staff will need to supply the following information for the sickness absence form (included at the end of this Policy statement):

❑   the nature of the illness or a broad indication of the cause of the absence;

❑   the anticipated length of absence.

2.5   Staff should make contact with their line manager regularly during the period of absence. For absences between one and seven consecutive days a

---

Figure 8.1   Example of a company Sickness Absence Policy Statement

self-certification form must be completed and signed by the individual upon their return to work. If the absence is likely to exceed seven days (including non-working days), the employee must obtain a medical certificate from a GP to cover the period of absence. This form must be forwarded to the employee's line manager as soon as possible. If the absence continues, medical certificates must be obtained to cover the whole period of absence. If the absence has exceeded six weeks the final certificate must contain the date on which the employee is deemed fit to return to work.

3.   Return to Work Following Sickness Absence

3.1   When staff return to work following a period of sickness absence they should report to their line manager as soon as possible. The individual will need to check and sign the absence record form and provide any doctor's certificates required covering their period of absence.

3.2   The line manager will discuss the reason(s) for absence with the member of staff. At the end of the meeting, the line manager will advise the individual what, if any, further action will be taken. The line manager will inform the Personnel Manager of the outcome of this meeting.

3.3   The sickness absence record is confidential and will be stored in the individual staff member's personnel file. The department manager will need to record the absence on the department's monthly absence record, which will be used for monitoring and further investigation as required.

4.   Monitoring Sickness Absence

4.1   Department managers are responsible for reviewing sickness absence to ensure that the department is able to function effectively. Records of absence should be checked for patterns of absence, which give cause for concern, including those that may be exacerbated by the working environment. If an individual's pattern of absence gives a manager cause for concern, the department manager should discuss this with them.

5.   Repeated Short-term Absence

5.1   The absence of a member of staff due to sickness for three periods of sickness in a rolling 12-month period, or a total of 10 or more working days within the same period, will trigger a formal Sickness Absence meeting between the individual and their line manager. This will depend on the reasons for absence. For instance, post-operative recuperation may require a period of absence exceeding the trigger period and would not lead to a formal Sickness Absence meeting.

5.2   A formal Sickness Absence meeting will normally take place when the trigger number of days absent has been reached. The individual will be given seven days' notice in writing of the date of the meeting and she/he may be

Figure 8.1   continued

accompanied by a trade union representative or a work colleague. The meeting will allow the individual and their line manager to discuss the record of absence, the reason(s) for it and where appropriate, to identify the improvement that is required over a specific time period.

5.3   If during any period of monitoring following the formal Sickness Absence meeting, an individual's absence exceeds the improvement target agreed, there will be a second formal Sickness Absence meeting with the Department Manager. If the pattern of sickness continues and the agreed attendance levels are not met following this second meeting, the discipline procedure will be invoked.

5.4   A member of staff who fails to comply with the notification and certification procedures may be subject to further action, which could include invoking the disciplinary procedure.

6.   Prolonged Sickness Absence

6.1   In cases of long-term absence of six weeks or more the department should maintain contact with the member of staff to keep up-to-date on the likely duration of the sickness absence. The individual has a responsibility to update his/her line manager regularly on his/her likely date of return to work.

6.2   If the member of staff is considered to be permanently unfit to resume his/her duties, re-design of work and an amendment to the job description may be considered. If this is not possible, re-deployment to another kind of work, where feasible, will be explored. The individual's views will be taken into account when exploring options. Following the meeting, any agreements and/or actions needed will be confirmed in writing.

6.3   If the member of staff is considered to be permanently unfit to return to work and redeployment is not possible, early retirement on the grounds of ill-health will be pursued. The Human Resource Manager will advise the individual of their entitlement under the company's pension scheme.

6.4   If an individual is deemed to be permanently unfit for employment and ill-health retirement is not possible, consideration will be given to termination of his/her employment. Following consultation, if termination is considered appropriate, confirmation in writing will be made by the Human Resource Manager. The right of appeal against the decision and the mechanism for appealing will be explained.

7.   Monitoring the Policy

7.1   Senior management will keep the monitoring of sickness absence and the operation of this policy under review. Any changes/adjustments made in the future will be communicated to all personnel by the Human Resource Manager.

Figure 8.1   continued

INDIVIDUAL ABSENCE REQUEST FORM

Name_____ Staff No._____

Department_____

I would like to request the following time off:

From:_____ To:_____

(include day, date and year)

If part of a day, state time:_____ am/pm

Reason for absence:
(Please tick appropriate box)

Annual leave	
Hospital attendance	
Appointment with doctor, clinic, dentist, other (please specify below)	
Jury duty	
Other (please specify below)	

Please complete if absence not approved in advance.

Dates absent_____

Reason(s)_____

Employee's signature_____ Date _____

Authorized by:

With pay	
Without pay	

Manager's signature_____Date_____

Figure 8.2   Example of an Individual Absence Request Form

Setting absence targets for line managers can help organizations to reduce the impact of absence on their business operations. Line managers usually know their staff well and are able to identify genuine instances of sickness or other legitimate absence. An initial, informal approach by the line manager can often cure the problem of occasional absence. However, in some persistent cases, formal procedures may need to be invoked, and disciplinary action may need to be taken.

It is important for all managers to understand how high levels of absence impact on service delivery. Absences cause disruption to production lines and service provision and create pressure for those workers who may be required to bridge the gap in cases of staff absence. Absence is also costly and it is necessary to reign in any ongoing instances of continuing absence by specific individuals.

In cases of long-term sickness, either the employee's line manager or the Personnel Manager will need to discuss the issues with the individual concerned and perhaps seek information from the company doctor or the individual's own General Practitioner.

It has been reported that up to 9 million of the 22 million requests for GP sick notes every year are bogus. It has also been suggested that twice as many men as women are willing to cheat the system.

Currently, a doctor's certificate is only provided after a period of seven days of illness. The most common reasons for seeking a GP's certificate relate to workplace stress, other stress-related problems and back problems. However, in contrast, it appears that when workers themselves are asked to identify the reasons for taking time off, among those cited include:

■ Emotional reasons – issues that they felt unable to discuss with their employer.
■ Stress caused by pressure at work.
■ A request for holiday being refused.
■ In some instances, individuals didn't want to use any of their holiday allocation.
■ Some perceive sick notes as a means of providing a legitimate reason to 'skive' off work.

For all periods of sickness of seven days or less, an employee should be expected to complete a self-certification form, which is usually part of an organization's Sickness and Absence Policy and Procedure. An example of a company's Sickness Absence Self-certification Form is detailed in Figure 8.3.

SICKNESS ABSENCE
SELF-CERTIFICATION FORM
(required for first seven days of absence, including non-working days)

Name:_____ Staff No:_____

Job Title:_____ Department: _____

Date and time illness began:_____
(include non-working days)

Name of person contacted: _____

Date and time of contact:_____

Reason(s) for absence:

Describe symptoms:

Did you visit your GP?   Yes/No
If 'No' did you visit a hospital, clinic or other medical establishment? Yes/No
If 'Yes' please identify and explain the reason(s).

Were you prescribed medication?   Yes/No

I understand that to provide inaccurate or false information regarding my absence will be treated as gross misconduct and could lead to my dismissal from the organization.

Signed: _____ Date: _____

Remarks:

Signed: _____ Date: _____
           Department Manager

Figure 8.3   Example of a Sickness Absence Self-certification Form

Organizations will need to develop appropriate documentation in order to manage and record sickness and other absence effectively. Figure 8.4 is an example of a Sickness Absence Record Form for

---

SICKNESS ABSENCE RECORD FORM

Name:_____ Department: _____

Contact telephone number : _____

Date of first absence: _____

Date/time of call informing of absence: _____

Date, time and content of follow-up calls:

Nature of illness: _____

Date returned to work: _____

Completed by: _____

Line manager

The following should be completed by the member of staff when s/he returns to work following a period of absence:

I confirm that the above information is correct and that I am fit and well to return to work today:

Signed _____

Name: _____
        (Please complete in block capitals)

Date of return to work: _____

This form to be handed to the Department Manager who will record the information and place the document in the individual's personnel file.

Figure 8.4   Example of a Sickness Absence Record Form

recording unexpected absence. Figure 8.5 is an example of a Monthly Departmental Absence Record. The period of reporting departmental absence will depend upon the organization's own absence control procedures. The report might be weekly or monthly. The example shown in Figure 8.5 could be used in either case. Figure 8.6 is an example of an Employee Absence Record Form for a 12-month period.

Employers use a diverse range of measures where absenteeism is high. Some employers have adopted measures that herald a return to those found in the Victorian era where the individual is expected to come to the office to sign to confirm that they are sick before being allowed to go home and take the day off.

More proactive organizations have adopted the 'return-to-work interview', which affords the opportunity to discuss with an individual the reasons why they were absent. On their return to work attempts are also made to ascertain whether the absence is likely to happen again.

There is no doubt that stress is a large cause of absenteeism across organizations in the United Kingdom and is particularly so in high-pressure environments.

There is a growing trend in organizations to discourage staff from taking time off even when they are genuinely unwell. Absence is perceived as weakness. Employees are often concerned that if they take time off this will affect their future prospects with the organization. The benefit to organizations of adopting this approach is difficult to identify. Individuals in this situation are likely to under-perform and this will also impact adversely on the performance of the organization.

Some larger organizations have found other ways of managing the problem. These include offering the opportunity to spend an allocated amount of time weekly to deal with home matters, and to offer flexible working arrangements to facilitate family needs. However, smaller organizations will find it difficult to adopt such approaches because of the limited number of staff available to them at any given time.

MONTHLY DEPARTMENTAL ABSENCE RECORD

Department _____   Month: _____

Employee Name	No. of Days Absent	Reason	Date Approved

Manager's signature: _____   Date: _____

Figure 8.5 Example of a Monthly Departmental Absence Record

EMPLOYEE ABSENCE RECORD

Name_____   Year_____

Department_____   Staff No. _____

Date employment commenced_____

Wk No	Mon	Tue	We	Th	Fri	Sat		Wk No	Mon	Tue	We	Th	Fri	Sat

Comments:

Key: S = Statutory sick pay   H = Holiday
      W = Waiting day   M = Maternity leave
      CS = Company sick pay   C = Compassionate leave
      X = No sick pay   L = Late

Figure 8.6 Example of an Employee Absence Record Form covering a 12-month period.

Absence levels are likely to reduce if an organization pays particular attention to ensuring that the working environment is clean and safe and that work is designed to be interesting and challenging. An appropriate reward system should be in situ and there should be good communications and employment relations evident within the organization. Implementing effective training and development also helps to reduce absenteeism.

Triggers for further investigation

The data that would trigger further investigation would be more helpful and more easily accessible if it was stored on a computer database. Using the data recorded, patterns of absence, together with reasons for absence, can be easily and regularly mapped by the relevant manager. The kind of information provided might include:

- How often has absence occurred and what was the period of time of each absence?
- What was the reason given for each of the absences?
- Was the absence covered by certification from a doctor?

This would allow a manager to identify recurring problems in either a particular department, section or in relation to a specific individual or individuals. This information would help the manager to consider whether further investigation is needed and what, if any, action should be taken.

A manager will need to consider the data carefully to ensure that misinterpretation does not occur. Should sudden changes occur in an individual's attendance patterns, then further investigation will be needed. It would not be appropriate to invoke disciplinary procedures without further investigation. A sudden personal problem may have occurred in the case of a particular individual and this may be impacting on their ability to attend work. In instances like these, consideration might be given to looking at more flexible working until matters have improved, or alternatively, counselling may be offered.

Every organization will identify specific criteria that will trigger further investigation. An organization might decide on a specified number of absences in a given period, or on a total number of absences.

A range of organizations use a diversity of triggers and the approach to be adopted will strongly depend on company policy. Some employers have stringent policies, which might specify for instance, two absences or six days off in a rolling one-year time frame. Others are less rigid, identifying five or six absences a year or five days in a period of one month. In some instances, acceptable levels of absence are agreed in negotiation with those trade unions that represent sectors of a company's workforce.

RETURN-TO-WORK INTERVIEWS

Return-to-work interviews, following an individual's period of absence from work, are more commonly used now than in the past. In organizations where this approach is adopted, levels of attendance are monitored, usually using computer-based systems, which 'trigger' areas where possible problems may be an issue. Information regarding absence levels tend to be circulated to senior managers and various strategies are introduced to deal with identified problems.

Return-to-work interviews assist organizations to identify the reasons for staff absence and to suggest or offer support where serious problems arise. They also afford an opportunity to point out to individuals that there should be a very good reason why they are unable to turn up for work. The implication is that attendance is expected unless there is a very good reason for not doing so.

The interview assists in generating an attendance culture where genuine illness is accepted but where inappropriate absence may well result in disciplinary procedures being invoked.

Preparing for and conducting the interview

As with any other interview, a return-to-work interview requires thorough preparation by the manager conducting the interview. Information that will be needed includes:

■   the individual's history of absence;
■   what was the reason for the individual's latest absence; and
■   any personal issues that may prove relevant.

The manager may seek information from a former line manager or supervisor and possibly a shop steward in cases where trade unions are active and recognized within the organization.

The interview

The interviewer should explain the purpose of the interview, and then use appropriate questioning techniques to identify relevant information. The approach should be serious but supportive and the exchange should be calm and considered. Solutions need to be identified that are agreed by both parties and an action plan should be produced that will be reviewed at an agreed time where relevant.

Follow-up

As in all interviews, follow-up action is important. The interviewer should write up notes straight away after the meeting and copies should be sent to the employee concerned and relevant managers. If serious issues have been identified, appropriate support should be offered to the individual.

Task

It is generally accepted practice that line/department managers should be responsible for their section's/department's absence management.

1. Does your organization have absence controls in place? If 'Yes', how do these compare with those outlined above?
2. Are there changes that could be made to improve the current systems?

Task

You are to take the role of Human Resource Manager. You have noticed a growing trend in short-term absences and your organization does not have absence procedures in situ currently.

1. Consider what kind of information you will need should you decide to introduce an absence control system.
2. Is this information currently available? If 'Yes', is this in an appropriate format?
3. What would be the most appropriate approach for you to take?
4. Outline the proposed process for introducing absence control measures within your own organization. You will need to consider:

   - what record systems are needed;
   - how information will be gathered;
   - how information will be disseminated to employees to ensure that it is understood;
   - how absence will be managed;
   - who will be responsible for implementing the process and monitoring its effectiveness;
   - how regularly you will review the process and make any necessary adjustments.

Scenario – absenteeism

One of the big four supermarkets has recently introduced new measures to tackle the problem of absenteeism. In an attempt to discourage absenteeism, the organization will not pay individuals for the first three days of sickness absence. The scheme is compulsory in new branches and voluntary in existing ones. The intention is to get individuals to consider carefully before taking time off.

The organization offers a choice of incentives.

1. An extra three days' holiday on top of normal annual leave entitlement, losing one day for each day of sickness absence.
2. Or, employees can earn vouchers for food for every 12-week period of work without absence.

The organization does offer flexible hours if absence is pre-arranged for personal appointments or family commitments.

One of the other top four supermarkets does not pay sick pay to hourly paid workers for the first three days of absence. It does, however, offer seven extra days' holiday and flexible hours for those who need time off for personal reasons, in an attempt to reduce absenteeism.

Some commentators have suggested that these measures may well encourage workers to take off longer periods of time to overcome the three-day rule.

Over the past 25 years, long-term sickness absence has doubled, with stress being identified as the major cause. GPs have conceded that it is difficult for them to confirm that the problems associated with stress are legitimate.

Task

Consider the strategies for managing absence identified in both the above scenario and the section on 'absence investigation'.

1. Which, if any, would you propose to adopt in order to reduce levels of absenteeism in your organization?
2. If none, what other strategies do you consider would better suit your particular organization?
3. What actions would you propose to take in order to implement your choice(s)?

Case study: Aztec Technical Services Ltd

Sickness and Absence Control Procedure – Main Principles

We will be implementing an Absence Control Procedure from 01 April 2005; the main principles and provisions of the procedure are listed below:

The Procedure is designed to:

- encourage a positive culture within the organization;
- ensure that absence receives the appropriate mix of concern and consideration for employees' welfare;
- establish consistent monitoring of trends and individual absence, and ensure that necessary follow-up action is taken where necessary;
- recognize the high cost of absenteeism and encourage line managers to reduce these costs by taking action on a sustained, fair and consistent basis;
- clarify roles and responsibilities in the organization in respect of the responsibilities of absence.

Absence Classification:

Short-term	Up to and including 5 days;
Medium-term	6 to 30 days (employee keeps in regular contact with the HR Department. Appointment with Company Doctor arranged after 20+ days of absence).
Long-term	31+ days (employee maintains regular contact with HR Department plus will be required to visit the Company Doctor on a regular basis).

Absence Notification. Employee Responsibilities are:

- Making initial contact with your manager within one half-hour of shift start time. This reporting procedure must be observed daily until sickness documentation is received or the number of days' absence is known and can be confirmed.
- Absences of up to seven calendar days (includes weekends) must be supported by a self-certification note (available from the HR Department) and thereafter by a doctor's sickness note.
- All initial sickness documentation must be received promptly and at the very latest, during the day of return.

HR/Management Action during Absence:

- Ascertain any new absences/update on medium and long-term absences/check any returns to work.

■ Analyse the employee's time and attendance record for the year to date (plus three-year data if appropriate) and make recommendations for review.

Returning to Work:

■ Your line manager will conduct a return-to-work interview.
■ It will give your line manager an opportunity to understand the reasons for your absence.
■ Ensures that correct procedures have been followed.
■ The return-to-work interview is an opportunity to discuss your previous absence and the importance of good attendance.
■ Identifies the requirement for future action if good attendance is not maintained.

Task

Review the Sickness and Absence Control Procedure for Aztec Technical Services Limited.

1. Is the procedure adequate to allow Aztec to monitor absence effectively?
2. In your opinion, will the procedure achieve the aims identified by Aztec? If not, what proposals would you put forward to strengthen the procedure for the future?

Case study: IT Systems Company

Following a sudden upturn in business, the IT Systems Company has found it necessary to introduce a new nightshift in the computer centre to cope with the increased workload.

Some new staff have been recruited, but three other members of staff, Harold Featherstone, Vijay Singh and Philip Brown, who are experienced with the system, have been transferred from the dayshift. All three expressed dissatisfaction at having to work nights.

Three weeks later, when work pressure was high, Featherstone failed to arrive for work. He phoned later to say that he was in bed with 'flu'.

That same night, there was a massive computer breakdown. Singh and Brown urgently made arrangements to complete the work on a subsidiary company's computer and travelled together in Brown's car. Passing through town, they thought they saw Featherstone outside a local restaurant.

Singh and Brown were discussing the evening's events when they returned to the office. Turning suddenly they found the Personnel Manager standing right behind them.

Task

You are the Personnel Manager of IT Systems Ltd. What action would you propose to take regarding Featherstone's absence?

Case study: Maggie Hewson (Part 1)

Maggie Hewson has worked on the production line at Freezerama Frozen Foods Ltd for 10 years. Maggie's timekeeping is exceptional and she has had only three days absence through illness during her employment with the company. She is hardworking and reliable.

However, during the past seven days, Maggie's line manager, Bill Friend, has noticed that she has been late for work every day by about four or five minutes.

Bill mentioned this to her two days ago and apparently although she seemed flustered, Maggie reassured him that she would be on time in future. Unfortunately, the lateness has continued.

Bill has approached the company's Personnel Manager for advice on how to proceed.

Task

You are to take the role of Personnel Manager at Freezerama Frozen Foods Ltd. You advise Bill that at this stage you don't feel that Maggie's lateness should be viewed as a disciplinary issue.

Assist Bill to prepare his case and identify the points you feel he should discuss with Maggie during the course of the informal meeting you have suggested he invite her to attend.

9

Discipline and grievance management

In any organization, there will be occasions when disputes arise between management and the workforce. In order that any disputes can be settled amicably and quickly it is necessary to devise ways of dealing with them.

When an employee has difficulties through actions taken by management, this generally results in the employee having a grievance. If, on the other hand, management has problems with the behaviour or actions of employees, this is an issue of discipline and may result in disciplinary action being taken against the employee concerned.

Procedures for the resolution of discipline and grievance issues are controlled by legislation. Discipline and grievance are issues that generally affect the individual, but it would be unfair to treat each individual differently. Therefore, it is necessary to develop procedures that can be applied fairly to all employees, regardless of status.

Handling disciplinary issues inappropriately can result in a claim for unfair dismissal against the organization. This could be costly, not only in terms of finance but also in other ways. Disputes can create negative publicity, which will in turn affect the company's image. Time will need to be allocated to prepare for any tribunal proceedings resulting from a dispute and there will also be disruption to work. Disputes also tend to impact on employee relations within the organization.

LEGISLATION

To comply with legislation and to ensure clarity all organizations must have a disciplinary procedure that conforms to the Employment Act 2002.

It is important to keep procedures simple but it is equally important that they comply with the Act. The standard procedures contained within the Act consist of three steps. Briefly, they are:

1. Where an employer invokes disciplinary action or dismissal against an employee, the employer must state the reasons in writing. A copy must be sent to the employee, and the employer must invite the employee to a meeting to discuss the issue(s).
2. This meeting must take place before any action is taken against the employee, and before suspension occurs. No meeting should take place before:

   - the employer has explained to the individual, the basis for the statement(s) contained within the written statement given under Step 1.
   - adequate time has been allowed for the individual to consider their response to the information.

   The individual must make every effort to attend the meeting, and after the meeting the organization must inform the individual of its decision and advise them of their right to appeal against the decision.
3. The individual must inform the organization if they wish to appeal. A further meeting must then be arranged by the organization and the individual concerned must make every effort to attend this. It is not necessary for the appeal meeting to occur before the disciplinary action or dismissal takes effect. Following the appeal meeting, the organization must inform the individual of its decision.

Organizations within the United Kingdom need to make themselves familiar with the Act to ensure that they instigate/revise procedures to conform to the legislation.

Dismissal procedures

The legislation introduced a 13-step procedure relating to cases of dismissal, which it has been suggested could cut down the number of tribunal cases arising from employees with a grievance. The 13 steps are:

1. Arguments for dismissal must be put in writing.
2. A letter must be sent to the relevant employee.
3. The employee should be given time to consider their response.
4. The employer should hold a meeting with the employee.
5. The employee should be allowed to explain their position.
6. Following the meeting, the employee should be advised of the decision taken.
7. The employee must be offered an opportunity to appeal against the decision.
8. The employee must be invited to a further meeting to discuss the appeal.
9. A senior officer of the company should be assigned to deal with any appeal.
10. The employee should be informed of the appeal decision made.
11. All meetings should be held at reasonable times.
12. All meetings should be held in reasonable locations.
13. The above stages must not be delayed unreasonably.

Failure of a company to follow procedure will result in an automatic ruling in favour of the employee. The rules also relate to cases of sex discrimination.

STRATEGIES FOR PREVENTION

To avoid disciplinary issues arising in the first place, the organization should consider adopting strategies that eliminate as far as feasible the likelihood of problems occurring. These could include for instance:

- effective induction and training and development programmes;
- job design – to ensure that individuals are not under-worked or over-worked;
- a clearly written down disciplinary procedure so that everyone knows exactly what is expected of them.

Appropriate disciplinary procedures should exist, which are written down and clearly explained to all employees at induction. The ground rules are then laid down and made clear from day one as to the likely outcome of any under-performance or unacceptable behaviour.

FEATURES OF A DISCIPLINARY PROCEDURE

In 1971, the Advisory Conciliation and Arbitration Service (Acas), produced a code of practice (*Disciplinary Practice and Procedures in Employment*), which identified essential features of any disciplinary procedure. The code was not binding but where there were no other procedures in situ, or where a procedure was poorly designed, it could be admissible in evidence to an industrial tribunal that was attempting to assess the fairness of dismissal.

The Acas code was designed to give practical advice on how to handle disciplinary issues effectively and it ensured that procedures were credible. Whilst the Acas code of practice has now been superseded by measures detailed in the Employment Act 2002, Acas has updated its code of practice, which will be useful in assisting organizations to produce appropriate disciplinary and grievance procedures. Contact details for Acas appear in the 'Useful Contacts' section at the end of this book.

Disciplinary procedures

When developing a disciplinary procedure, it is useful to involve line managers, trade union representatives and other individuals from within the organization to ensure that procedures are developed that are fair and equitable.

There are many ways of handling disciplinary issues but it is also important that these are dealt with quickly and effectively if disruption is to be avoided.

Appeals

There should be a section within the disciplinary procedure that explains how an individual can appeal against a decision.

Records

Records of oral, written and final written warnings should be recorded on an individual's personnel file. These may be retained for specific periods identified by the organization. An oral and written warning may be kept on record for three months while a final written warning may be kept on record for six months. Once the time has elapsed, and providing the individual has committed no further offence, the record should be removed from their personnel file.

Examples of a written warning and final written warning letter are shown in Figures 9.1 and 9.2.

DISCIPLINARY OFFENCES

It would be difficult to identify a full range of behaviour that would result in disciplinary action being taken. The most common relate to bad timekeeping, absenteeism and poor work performance. There are likely to be others that relate to health and safety, theft, obeying rules and regulations, sexism and racism. Others may be in relation to behaviour such as threatening someone or fighting on premises. Alcohol and drug abuse are also issues that are cited.

Date

Name

Address

Dear Fred,

Written Warning

You attended a disciplinary interview on ____(date)_____ and were accompanied by your trade union representative. At the interview, it was decided that you would be given a written warning because of your persistent poor timekeeping. Prior to this, you had already received an oral warning on _____(date)_____, but there has been no improvement since this date.

You were warned that if your timekeeping did not improve during the following four-week period, we would have no alternative but to enter into the next stage of the company's disciplinary procedure and issue a written warning to you. You were advised that this written warning would stay on your personnel record for the next three months.

You have the right to appeal against this decision, by writing to _____(name)_____ within five days of receiving this letter.

Yours sincerely

Trevor Banks
Manager – Packing Department

Figure 9.1   An example of a Written Warning letter

Disciplinary offences are usually split into those that are regarded as gross misconduct, and those that are disciplinary offences. These offences may be handled differently depending upon the seriousness of the offence.

Gross misconduct

Each organization will decide on what is to be identified as 'gross misconduct' within the parameters of their operation. It is impossible to

---

Date

Name

Address

Dear Fred,

Final Written Warning

You attended a disciplinary interview on _____(date)_____ in the presence of your line manager and your trade union representative. At this disciplinary interview it was decided to issue you with this final written warning, which relates to your consistently poor timekeeping. You had previously received an oral warning on _____(date)____ and a written warning on _____(date)____.

Since these warnings were issued there has been no improvement in your timekeeping. You are now being issued with a final written warning and if there is no improvement in your timekeeping during the next four weeks, this will result in your dismissal from employment with us.

This warning will be filed on your personnel record and will be kept for a period of three months. You have a right to appeal against this decision by writing to the undersigned within five days of receipt of this warning letter.

Yours sincerely

Sally Richards
Human Resource Manager

Figure 9.2   An example of a Final Written Warning letter

produce a comprehensive list of all aspects of behaviour that would be classed as gross misconduct, but each organization should attempt to list as many as possible.

A procedure might include the following as gross misconduct and state that if any employee is found guilty of committing any of these offences, dismissal will result:

- theft of company property;
- deliberate damage to company property;
- fighting or other physical assault on company premises;

- fraud;
- incapacity due to abuse of drugs or alcohol;
- sexual harassment;
- racial harassment;
- gross infringement of health and safety rules and regulations.

This list is not exhaustive and there may be other offences that may be classed as gross misconduct. It would be appropriate to identify the company's stance on convictions for criminal activity. Being convicted of a criminal offence committed external to the company may result in dismissal but this may not be an automatic reason for dismissing an individual. Consideration should be given to the type of work carried out by the individual and whether the nature of the offence will impact on his/her suitability to carry on doing the job. It is usual to suspend such individuals on full pay until a full investigation is carried out.

UNFAIR DISMISSAL

The concept of unfair dismissal was first introduced by the Industrial Relations Act 1971, which later became the Employment Protection (Consolidation) Act 1978 and in later legislation. An industrial tribunal must make the decision as to whether a dismissal is fair or unfair.

There are five potentially 'fair' reasons within the Act:

- a reason related to the capability (including health) or qualifications of an employee for performing the work he/she was employed to do;
- reasons related to the employee's conduct;
- that the employee was redundant;
- that the employee could not continue to work in the position that he/she held without contravention (on the part of him/her or the employer) of a duty or restriction imposed under a legal instrument;

■ some other substantial reason of a kind to justify dismissal of an employee holding the position that the employee held (eg, reorganization).

FORMAL DISCIPLINARY PROCEDURE

A disciplinary procedure should usually be set out in writing and include the essential elements identified previously in this chapter. The sections of the procedure will usually include:

1. the scope and purpose of the procedure(s);
2. the underlying principles on which the procedure is based;
3. stages in the process;
4. identification of what behaviour/actions are considered to be 'gross misconduct';
5. how an individual can appeal against any decision taken by management.

Figure 9.3 shows the content of one company's disciplinary procedure. This is for a garden centre and farm shop operation, which employs 17 full-time and 54 part-time staff and is the only branch operated by this particular organization.

GRIEVANCE PROCEDURE

Grievances relate to those instances when problems arise between management and an employee. When the relationship that exists between an organization and its employee is unsatisfactory to the employee, then that person has a grievance. Grievance processes relate to an individual employee's problems except where collective agreements exist. Grievances can cause disruption, particularly where issues are not resolved. The size and nature of the organization will dictate the type of procedures that are in situ to deal with such occurrences.

The Green Wellie Garden Centre and Farm Shop

DISCIPLINARY PROCEDURE

Sub-section 1 – General

These procedures will apply to **ALL** employees of The Green Wellie Garden Centre and Farm Shop.

The disciplinary actions outlined in these procedures will be invoked when all efforts have failed to assist the employee in meeting the Company's requirements.

Employees are expected to carry out and comply with any reasonable instructions or requests made by their Manager, his/her superiors or his/her nominee.

Employees may be suspended on full pay at any stage of the Disciplinary Procedure, or at any time that is considered appropriate by management.

The right to be accompanied within the Disciplinary Procedure is restricted to a fellow employee or union representative who may attend any interview(s) as a witness to the proceedings.

If an employee is disciplined or dismissed in accordance with these procedures, confirmation of the decision will be forwarded to the individual in writing within three days of the interview taking place and will be deemed to be effective from the date of the disciplinary interview.

Details of how to appeal against a decision appear later within this document.

Sub-section 2 – Procedure

Stage 1 – Formal Verbal Warning

If you act in breach of your terms and conditions of employment or if your conduct or performance is unsatisfactory you will be given a Formal Verbal Warning in the first instance.

Your manager will normally give this Formal Verbal Warning to you. Formal Verbal Warnings will remain current for a period of six months.

If your conduct or performance is of particular concern then your manager will have the right to move immediately to Stage 2 of the Procedure and will not therefore issue a Formal Verbal Warning.

Figure 9.3   Disciplinary Procedure Statement for The Green Wellie Garden Centre and Farm Shop

---

The Green Wellie Garden Centre and Farm Shop

DISCIPLINARY PROCEDURE (continued)

Though not exhaustive, listed below are examples likely to attract Verbal Warnings:

- ❏ persistent lateness;
- ❏ absenteeism;
- ❏ disregard for personal appearance and/or hygiene;
- ❏ poor job performance;
- ❏ minor insubordination.

Stage 2 – Written or Final Written Warnings

Should you fail to make the required improvement in performance, or if there is a further incidence of misconduct or breach of Conditions of Employment, you will be interviewed by your Manager. You will be informed of the complaints made against you and will be given the opportunity of stating your case. At this interview you will have the right to be accompanied by a fellow employee of your choice.

If the Manager conducting the interview is not satisfied with your explanation, you will receive a Formal Written Warning outlining the disciplinary action that will follow further offences or failure to improve.

This Warning will be confirmed in writing within three days of the interview taking place, and will be deemed to be effective from the date of the Disciplinary Interview.

The seriousness of the offence will determine whether a Written Warning or Final Written Warning is issued. Written or Final Written Warnings will remain current for a period of six months.

Though not exhaustive, listed below are examples likely to attract a Written or a Final Written Warning:

- ❏ repetition of a previous offence(s);
- ❏ rudeness to customers or colleagues;
- ❏ smoking in NO SMOKING areas;
- ❏ conduct prejudicial to the good name of the Company;
- ❏ abuse of the staff purchase facility;

Figure 9.3 continued

The Green Wellie Garden Centre and Farm Shop

DISCIPLINARY PROCEDURE (continued)

- ❏ gambling whilst on duty or on the Company premises;
- ❏ misuse of, or unauthorized use of a fork lift truck;
- ❏ refusal to carry out a reasonable instruction given by your Supervisor;
- ❏ refusal to wear protective clothing and/or the Company's uniform as required;
- ❏ sexual harassment;
- ❏ unlawful discrimination;
- ❏ a breach of Health & Safety Rules & Regulations;
- ❏ drinking during the day, which may cause offence to customers or staff.

Stage 3 – Dismissal

If the required improvement does not result from the Written Warning, or if further misconduct occurs, the following procedure will be instigated:

3.1 You will receive a letter that details the reasons for your dismissal.

3.2 You will be given 10 working days to consider your response.

3.3 You will then be invited to a disciplinary interview, which will be conducted by your line manager. Your trade union representative or one other person of your choice may accompany you.

3.4 You will have the opportunity to explain your position at this meeting.

3.5 Following the meeting, you will be advised of the decision within three working days.

3.6 You will have the opportunity to appeal against the decision made. Refer to the Appeals Procedure.

3.7 The Director responsible for Personnel will meet with you to hear your appeal.

3.8 You will be informed of the outcome of your appeal within three working days of the appeal hearing.

Figure 9.3　continued

The Green Wellie Garden Centre and Farm Shop

DISCIPLINARY PROCEDURE (continued)

Sub-section 3 – Gross misconduct

In the case of gross misconduct, you will be subject to Summary Dismissal without notice or any prior warning. In addition you will forfeit all benefits you may have accumulated at the time of dismissal.

You may be suspended at any time on full pay until a full investigation has been carried out and the appropriate manager has interviewed you. At this interview you will be informed of the complaint against you and will be given the opportunity to examine the evidence, or hear verbal evidence against you. At this meeting you may be accompanied by a fellow employee of your choice.

If, as a result of this Investigatory Interview the manager believes there is a case to answer, a Disciplinary Hearing will be arranged. At this meeting you may be accompanied by a fellow employee of your choice.

At the Disciplinary Hearing, if it is decided that you are to be dismissed, your dismissal will be confirmed by letter within three days of the interview taking place, specifying the reason(s) for dismissal. You will be advised verbally at this interview that you have been dismissed and of your Right of Appeal. A senior manager will hear your appeal and the appeal decision will be advised to you in writing within three working days of the appeal taking place.

Though not exhaustive, listed below are examples of Gross Misconduct:

- ❏ personal misconduct, which may give offence to any other employee or customer and which may be in breach of civil or criminal law, or which breaches the trust that needs to exist between the Company and its employee;
- ❏ negligence and/or a deliberate failure to comply with the Company's Safety Rules;
- ❏ deliberately making false statements, or dishonest conduct in relation to the Company, its employees, customers or suppliers;
- ❏ misappropriation or unauthorized possession of Company monies, property or the monies or property belonging to any other Company employee, customer or supplier;
- ❏ serious breaches of Company operating procedures or any serious breach of security;

Figure 9.3   continued

The Green Wellie Garden Centre and Farm Shop

DISCIPLINARY PROCEDURE (continued)

❏ having consumed excessive alcoholic beverages that results in an employee's inability to carry out their duties effectively;

❏ anti-social activity such as brawling, indecency, physical violence or assault at the place of work;

❏ vandalism or sabotage of the Company's premises, fixtures, equipment or stock;

❏ fitting and/or installing any of the Company's merchandise or products at a customer's premises for payment or reward.

Sub-section 4 – Appeals

If you consider that the disciplinary action taken against you is unreasonable, you may appeal by writing to the General Manager/Director within five working days of receipt of your disciplinary letter.

Appeals will be acknowledged promptly and arranged within 14 days or as soon as is reasonably practical thereafter.

You are entitled to be accompanied by an employee of your choice when attending the appeal hearing.

The result of the Appeal will be notified to you in writing within three working days of the Appeal Hearing. This decision will be final.

Figure 9.3   continued

In some circumstances, it should be possible to resolve grievances on an informal basis, but an individual may decide to invoke formal procedures, particularly where there is a perception of unfair treatment. Some grievances may appear trivial whilst others will be serious enough to need to be raised formally.

Some grievance issues may relate to a collective group of employees, perhaps relating to rates of pay or working conditions. Trade union representatives, who will negotiate with management collectively on behalf of their members, will usually take up collective grievance issues.

Some individuals will find it necessary to raise a grievance and it is necessary that these individuals know how they can do this formally. They need to know that the grievance will be dealt with fairly and that the outcome will be decided quickly.

The terms and conditions of employment under which an individual is employed should specify to whom an individual should report any grievance. During any grievance interview, the employee has the right to be accompanied by an individual of their choice. This could be a trade union official, work colleague or other person chosen by the employee.

Grievances can arise for a variety of reasons, which might include discrimination, victimization by management, sexual harassment, bullying, health and safety issues and changes in terms and conditions of employment, for instance.

Formal procedures assist the organization in being transparent in its dealings with grievance issues. It is important that organizations are seen to be treating all employees fairly regardless of their place within the structure of the organization.

The grievance procedure should be in writing and should be made available to all employees and may be contained within a Staff Handbook. Grievances should be dealt with quickly and fairly and managers should be trained to be able to deal with grievance issues.

Organizations vary in their nature and structure and every organization will have a different approach to developing and introducing formal procedures. Individuals who might be involved in any process can vary. These might be for instance: the personnel or human resource manager, the department manager, and a director. In terms of unions, this might be an individual, a shop steward or a full-time union official. Figure 9.4 details the grievance procedure for The Green Wellie Garden Centre and Farm Shop.

If there was no grievance procedure to deal with issues such as health and safety or harassment, then serious repercussions could arise. Grievance procedures provide an opportunity to resolve issues before they get out of control.

The Green Wellie Garden Centre and Farm Shop
GRIEVANCE PROCEDURE

Sub-section 1 – General

With the exception of disciplinary or dismissal matters, all grievances will be dealt with in the following way:

1. All grievances will be actioned as quickly as possible and every endeavour will be made by all parties to find a solution to the issue(s) raised.
2. An employee raising a grievance through procedure is entitled to be accompanied by a fellow employee of their choice.

Collective Grievance

In the first instance, collective grievances will be raised with the appropriate manager or through staff meetings.

If the matter is not resolved the manager will refer the matter to the General Manager in writing.

The General Manager will respond in writing within five days of receipt and his/her decision will be final.

Sub-section 2 – Procedure

Stage 1

Step 1

Any employee who has a grievance or feels that he/she has been unfairly treated will, in the first instance, raise the matter with his/her manager.

Step 2

A meeting will be arranged with your line manager during which you will be able to explain your concerns. A decision will made and any follow-up action instigated following this meeting.

Stage 2

If the matter remains unresolved, then a further meeting will be convened with your line manager who will be accompanied by the General Manager. This meeting will be arranged within five working days of the request for a further meeting.

You will be informed in writing of the decision that has been made within five days of the meeting taking place.

Figure 9.4   Grievance Procedure Statement for The Green Wellie Garden Centre and Farm Shop

Task

Do both disciplinary and grievance procedures exist within your organization?

1. If 'Yes', do these conform to the statutory requirements laid down by the Employment Act?
2. If not, take this opportunity to review the documentation included in this chapter and within the legislation and either:
   - make appropriate revisions to your current documentation;
   - or generate appropriate discipline and grievance procedures.
3. Decide how you will communicate these changes to all your employees.

Case study: The Crumbly Biskit Company

The Crumbly Biskit Company is a small family-run biscuit manufacturer employing approximately 200 people.

During the past few weeks some pilfering has been occurring and the Managing Director, in conjunction with his managers, has decided that every possible measure should be taken to find the culprit(s).

Working after normal hours one evening, Philip Strong, the Production Manager hears a noise as he leaves the shop floor. On investigation, he finds Melvin Forrester putting an expensive box of biscuits under his overcoat. Melvin, a father of three, is a loyal and hardworking employee who has been with the company since leaving school.

The following morning Strong reports the incident to the Personnel Manager.

Task

Adopt the role of the Personnel Manager at The Crumbly Biskit Company.

1. Identify the issues.
2. Prepare a list of questions you will wish to ask Forrester during the course of a scheduled disciplinary interview.

Case study: Melville & Company

Bill Entwistle is employed in the buying department of Melville & Company. Throughout his five years' service he has proved to be responsible, hardworking and extremely popular, and he stands out as having promotion potential.

Justin Mitchell, the Chief Buyer, promoted Entwistle to leader of the progress section. When he was notified of his promotion, Entwistle took his colleagues for a celebration drink. He and a number of others returned late, worse for drink, and interrupted the afternoon's work in all sections of the open-plan office. Mitchell had always maintained a strict timekeeping rule and was standing in the office on Entwistle's return.

Task

Adopt the role of the Human Resource Manager at Melville & Company. Justin Mitchell has approached you to ask for advice on how he should proceed.

1. Identify the specific issues that you think should be raised with Bill Entwistle.
2. What action would you advise Mitchell to take relating to each of the issues you have identified?

Case study: Dundown Ltd

Gary Moss has been a gas fitter with Dundown Ltd for eight years. He is an average worker, liked by his colleagues, but rather highly strung in temperament.

His supervisor, Fred Jones, considered a fair boss by his staff, is under a bit of pressure just now, due to a series of customer complaints and a heavy workload.

On Wednesday morning Gary asked Fred for the afternoon off to visit his young son in hospital. Fred was in a bit of a fix because his two best fitters were off sick. Then the phone rang. It was the installation manager asking Fred to go over immediately to discuss two serious complaints that had just been reported. Fred, looking worried, explained to Gary, and said, 'I'll see you later'. Then he rushed off and was with his boss until early afternoon.

Next morning, Marlon Campbell, a fitter who'd been on holiday for the past two days, was in early. He was talking to Fred about the match the previous afternoon and blurted out, 'Gary got real excited when the third goal was scored'.

Task

You are the Personnel Manager at Dundown Ltd. Fred has approached you for advice on how to proceed. Fred has confided in you that he is uncomfortable invoking the disciplinary procedure in this case.

1. Identify the issues and identify the advice you would give to Fred in these circumstances.
2. Consider your own organization's disciplinary procedure. Would this be adequate to allow you to deal with a similar matter appropriately and legally?

Case study: The Scrumptious Bakery

You are the Human Resource Manager at the Scrumptious Bakery. Some months ago, Paul Westwood was appointed as the new Sales Supervisor to take responsibility for a Van Sales team of 25 people.

Jack Fielding is a member of the Van Sales team who has been with the bakery for about two years. His sales figures are not the lowest in the group, but his round is usually among the bottom three.

The previous Sales Supervisor wasn't too enthusiastic about Jack and had said to you during the previous appraisal review, 'Jack's all right, but he's certainly not one of the best in my team. He seems to lack enthusiasm and he's been late several times'.

As HR Manager, you passed on information about performance etc of each individual within the Van Sales team when you briefed Westwood on his appointment.

Westwood has noticed that although Fielding keeps his van reasonably clean and is fairly cooperative, he always seems to be slow. He has a history of lateness and in fact, last Monday he was 25 minutes late and blamed the heavy traffic. Westwood accepted this explanation.

Fielding's approach to customers is satisfactory, but some of them are showing signs of impatience with his slow ways. It's difficult to put a finger on anything specific, but Westwood feels that there would be no problem if only he would liven up a bit. Westwood has mentioned this to Jack, but not in a very definite way. Now, however, Westwood feels that the time has come when something must be done about it.

Task

Is this a disciplinary issue at The Scrumptious Bakery?

1. If you decide that it is a disciplinary issue, what course of action would you advise Paul Westwood to take?
2. If you decide that this is not a disciplinary issue, how would you propose that Westwood deal with the issues identified in this case?

Case study: Maggie Hewson (Part 2)

To remind you from Chapter 8:

Maggie Hewson has worked on your production line for 10 years. Maggie is always on time, has had only three days' absence through illness during her employment with you. She is hardworking and reliable.

On your advice, Maggie's line manager, Bill Friend, held an informal meeting with her recently to discuss her lateness. During that meeting with Maggie, Bill was unable to get to the bottom of why her timekeeping has been problematic recently.

At the time, Bill suggested that he would be willing to adjust her hours of work for a short period of time if this would help her situation. She had thanked him but had reassured him that she would make sure that she would arrive on time in future. Because of her reliability, Bill decided to accept her assurances.

However, during the past two weeks the lateness has continued. Bill cannot afford to let this continue because Maggie's lateness is causing disruption to production.

Task

You are the Personnel Manager and Bill has approached you once again for advice on how he should proceed. He doesn't want to lose Maggie because of her commitment and hard work when she is on-site. However, he feels very strongly that the disruption to production can't continue either.

You have decided to advise Bill to deal with Maggie's continuing lateness by invoking the company's discipline procedure.

1. Prepare your case and identify the points that you suggest Bill should discuss with Maggie during the course of the disciplinary meeting.
2. Following Bill's meeting with Maggie, he advises you that he has gleaned a good deal of information about Maggie's current personal circumstances. (See the background to this case, which appears at the end of this chapter.)
3. What course of action would you propose that Bill should take in these circumstances?
4. Would Maggie's personal problems have influenced your advice to Bill regarding what action to take if you had been aware of them?

Case study: Tyrone Miller's suit

Tyrone Miller is a paint representative with the One Coat Paint Company and has been on the road for 15 years. His sales figures for most of that time have been better than those of his 10 colleagues, although recently he's slipped to third place.

Yesterday, a drizzly day, Miller was travelling from Birmingham to Chester, but made a detour of a total of 15 miles to call on an old friend. After he'd left to continue his calls, his company car skidded into a wall, which slightly damaged the front. Some sample tins of paint he was carrying on the back seat burst open at the moment of impact, and splashed his suit beyond hope of dry cleaning.

On his return to the office that day, Miller claimed the cost of a new suit on the grounds that the cans must have been inadequately sealed. It was normal company practice to allow small detours in the employee's own time. On this occasion, Miller had spent about an hour with his friend, and had had a couple of pints of bitter with him.

Task

You are to take the role of Personnel Manager.

1. Identify the issues in the Tyrone Miller case study.
2. What actions would you propose to take?

Background to the Maggie Hewson case study

Maggie's daughter had split up from her husband of three years and she had a baby of nine months. Maggie was in something of a state about how things might work out. Her daughter had arrived on her doorstep three weeks ago with the baby in her arms carrying only the baby's holdall and the clothes she stood up in. Amy, Maggie's daughter, had had a blazing row with her husband Tom and she had walked out. Maggie knew that the relationship had not been an easy one since the baby arrived. Tom was out of work and there was little money coming into the house to pay the bills and mortgage.

Maggie had thought that after a day or two, her daughter would return home and she could get back to some kind of normality. The house looked like a bomb had hit it. There were toys, clothes, empty mugs and dirty plates in every room. The kitchen looked like a hurricane had passed through it recently and it was all getting a little too much for Maggie. She loved her daughter dearly but she wasn't coping well with this new disruption to her tidy, ordered home. To cap it all, Maggie and

Amy had had a row that very morning and Maggie had left for work feeling flustered and upset.

She had arrived late for work every day since her daughter had descended on her doorstep and her supervisor had already had a word with her about her lateness. She had promised to be on time in future, but the chaos at home was making it impossible to keep that promise. Maggie was reluctant to 'air her dirty washing in public' and was reluctant to confide in anyone at work, including her supervisor, who had always been polite and courteous, but Maggie had never been close to anyone at the plant. She did her job and got paid and that's what she preferred.

10

Accident investigation

In the 1970s legislation was introduced that made management responsible for making provision for appropriate safety standards and policies, and to ensure that these were maintained over time. Intrinsic within this was the requirement to promote safety awareness and to introduce schemes, which were industry specific in some instances.

Generally within common law, all employers have a duty of care to protect their employees. It is now necessary to provide an environment within which employees are able to work safely. In addition, the employer must ensure that systems, plant and equipment are adequate and safe to use. For their part, employees have a duty to ensure that they carry out their duties safely and contribute to developing a safe working environment.

LEGISLATION

The Health and Safety at Work Act 1974 (HSWA) covers all places of work and states that employers should take all reasonable steps to ensure that the workplace is safe and that adequate welfare facilities are provided.

The HSWA has been updated and extended to include various regulations, codes of practice and guidance on a wide range of health and safety issues.

Employers' obligations

Within The Workplace (Health, Safety and Work) Regulations 1992, minimum standards for workplaces were identified:

- providing a clean workplace where all waste is cleared regularly;
- providing appropriate lavatories in readily accessible places;
- maintaining a reasonable temperature and provision of thermometers;
- maintaining the environment, equipment and systems;
- ensuring there is adequate ventilation;
- ensuring there is adequate floor space.

Inspectors from the Environmental Health Department of the local authority, or from the Health and Safety Executive are charged with enforcing the legislation. All workplaces must be registered with one of these bodies and employees can report breaches of health and safety and/or seek advice from them.

All employers must take out Employer's Liability Insurance to cover the potential for workplace accidents or work-related disease. The certificate should be displayed in a prominent place. Failure to take out insurance can result in a fine.

All organizations must take measures to ensure that fire risk is reduced as far as possible and must provide fire escape routes. There must also be a certificate from the local fire authority and employers must train employees in fire procedures and carry out regular escape drills. Since October 2003, legislation has provided the opportunity for employees to make civil claims against employers where illness or injuries occur due to a fire at work.

ACCIDENTS AT WORK

Accidents in the workplace may, or may not cause death, injury, damage or loss. It is crucial to investigate all accidents at work to try to ensure that there is no recurrence, by improving procedures and/or environments. Under health and safety legislation, the organization has a duty to investigate all accidents, and information gathered will also be needed for any issues that may arise in relation to insurance.

Research carried out by the Health and Safety Executive has concluded that approximately 70 per cent of accidents in the workplace occur through failures of management. Shortcomings identified included:

- The lack of adequate training in how to use equipment and what procedures should be followed in the case of an accident occurring.
- There was inadequate supervision to ensure that procedures and policies were carried out effectively.
- There was inadequate information available regarding the levels of risk and about how to prevent or control them.

It may be useful to record details of an accident on a document created for this purpose (see Figure 10.1). This would be useful not only for insurers but also for those accidents that have to be reported to the agencies responsible for enforcing health and safety within the workplace.

Ideally, all accidents should be subject to some investigation. It is then easier to spot any trends, even in minor injuries, and be able to instigate measures to eliminate or reduce the occurrence of such incidents. It is crucial to investigate all accidents that result in absence from work.

Both direct and indirect causes of accidents should be investigated. Some indirect causes of accidents might be lack of knowledge and/or skills to carry out a task; a failure to follow a procedure; inadequate maintenance of plant and equipment, etc. Examples of direct causes of accidents would be failure to use protective equipment where this is required and provided; using defective equipment etc.

Investigating an accident

Accident investigators should be open-minded and objective. Accidents should be investigated as soon as possible after they occur. It is sensible to ensure that the accident site is left undisturbed until a full investigation can take place.

COMPANY ACCIDENT RECORD

Name: _____ Staff No: _____

Department: _____ Job Title: _____

Home Address: _____

_____ Age: _____ Sex: _____

Date and time of accident: _____

Location of accident: _____

Witness(es):

How did the accident occur?

Injuries sustained:

Was any action taken immediately?

What was the cause of accident?

Per injured employee   Per witness(es)

When the accident occurred

1. Was the employee carrying out normal duties?   Yes/No
2. Did the work being carried out require protective clothing?   Yes/No
    If 'Yes', was the employee wearing the protective clothing?   Yes/No
3. Was the employee following correct procedures in carrying
    out the work?   Yes/No
    Please provide details on the reverse of this form if the answer to any of
    the above questions is 'No'.
4. Is the employee able to continue to work?   Yes/No

Any comments or recommendations

Signed: _____ Date: _____

Job Title: _____

Figure 10.1   A Company Accident Report form

It may be necessary to investigate serious accidents from time to time. However, the section below provides a practical accident investigation checklist, which should be appropriate for the majority of accidents that occur in an organization.

The cost of accidents in the workplace is difficult to assess but the HSE has identified some interesting facts. The cost to employers of injuries sustained at work is around £1 billion per year. In addition, the cost of absence through ill health caused through work is more than £1.5 billion a year.

An accident investigation checklist

Not all of the following will be relevant in all investigations. There may also be additional elements of the process that may need to be included for specific industries:

1. Try to establish the facts as quickly as possible after an accident has occurred. Witnesses should be identified at this time and notes made of environmental conditions, systems of work and equipment. The sequence of events that led up to the accident occurring, should also be established.
2. If possible, take photographs of the scene or draw a sketch and make notes of relevant measurements, as appropriate.
3. Interview all individuals involved in the accident and anyone who saw or heard anything that was related to the incident.
4. If liquids or other substances are involved, it may be necessary to gather samples for analysis.
5. When all information is collated, the data must be analysed to identify consistencies or inconsistencies. Inconsistencies will require further investigation.
6. Only when all the facts have been gathered and analysed can a conclusion about what caused the accident be identified.
7. Copies of all documents, including sketches and/or photos should be kept safely so that these can be referred to in the future if required.
8. All information should be forwarded to the organization's Safety Officer or Manager responsible for this aspect of company operations.

POLICIES AND PROCEDURES

Companies that employ five or more people must have a written statement on health and safety at work and must communicate this to their employees. Failure to provide written information is an offence and can result in a maximum fine of £20,000 in a Magistrates Court or an unlimited fine in a Crown Court. Employers must keep up-to-date with changes in health and safety legislation. The main issues that need to be included in a policy document are:

- the provision of relevant information regarding health and safety issues and how this will be communicated;
- adequate notice of changes to working practices or procedures;
- ensuring that policies are applied consistently across the working environment;
- exploration of ways in which the working environment can be improved;
- ensuring the system is monitored and reviewed regularly and that the policy is updated as and when required.

Consultation must be carried out before any changes are made in matters relating to health and safety and any information from suppliers, manufacturers etc, regarding safe use of products should also be communicated to employees.

Task

Does your organization have a policy and procedure for investigating industrial accidents?

1. If 'Yes', review the current procedure and documentation and make revisions where necessary.
2. If 'No', develop an appropriate procedure and relevant documentation and decide how you would propose to communicate this to all employees.

Health and safety representatives

In organizations where trade unions are recognized, the unions may appoint as many health and safety representatives as are needed to cover the number of employees adequately. By law, representatives can investigate complaints, accidents and dangerous occurrences, in addition to the workplace, when new equipment, working methods or materials are introduced. They are entitled by law to inspect the workplace at least once every three months.

These representatives are entitled to paid time off to attend training courses and to a desk, telephone etc, to allow them to carry out their duties adequately. Safety representatives can request a safety committee to be set up, whose function it will be to formulate policies and develop working practices that ensure employees' health and safety.

Training

Employers must ensure that their employees are trained adequately in health and safety issues. Initial training should take place when an employee joins the company as part of the induction training process. Ongoing training will be required should new equipment and/or new working practices be introduced.

Assessing risk

The Health and Safety At Work Regulations 1992 require companies to carry out regular assessments of the health and safety risks inherent within their organization in relation to their employees, visitors, agency staff, customers etc, and to instigate appropriate control measures.

Risk assessment can be carried out in relation to:

- Workstations – relating to the use of personal computers.
- Noise levels.
- Audits to assess potential hazards.

■   Lifting and handling heavy loads.
■   Special measures relating to risk assessment of pregnant women should also be carried out. If risks cannot be eliminated, a female employee must be found suitable alternative work, or be suspended on full pay to prevent exposure to hazards. Failure of the company in this area of risk assessment can lead to claims for sex discrimination.

Accidents and disease at work

Within The Reporting of Injuries, Diseases and Dangerous Occurrences Regulations 1995 (RIDDOR), it is laid down that employers must report any of the following to the HSE or local council at once:

■   dangerous occurrences;
■   accidents that prove fatal;
■   accidents where major injury occurs where medical treatment is required.

Other issues, which should be reported immediately by telephone and followed up by submitting a written report within seven days, are:

■   accidents that prevent an individual from carrying out their duties for a period of more than three days;
■   certain gas-related incidents;
■   some work-related diseases (infections, poisoning, lung diseases and other conditions linked to particular types of work).

First aiders must be provided by all organizations and employees should be made aware of how they can access first aid help when required.

All workplace injuries and accidents must be recorded in an Accident Book. The type of information to be recorded and kept for a period of three years is identified in the next section.

Accident investigation record-keeping

The responsible person must keep specific records and these must be retained for at least three years from the date on which they were made.

In the case of a reportable accident or dangerous occurrence:

- date and time of accident/dangerous occurrence;
- full name and occupation of person affected, including nature of injury or other condition;
- place where the accident/dangerous occurrence happened;
- brief description of the circumstances.

In the case of a reportable disease:

- date and time the disease was discovered;
- occupation of the person affected;
- name or nature of the disease.

Records must be kept at the place of work to which they refer.

Minor injuries

In addition, employers must ensure that all injuries, however minor, are recorded in an Accident Book, kept at a central location on the premises. The Accident Book is required under the Social Security (Claims and Payments) Regulations 1979 for all premises covered by the Factories Act 1961 or where 10 or more persons are employed at any time.

Accident Book

The book must be in a form approved by the Secretary of State for Social Services and contain the following information:

- full name, address and occupation of injured person;
- date and time of accident;

- place where accident happened;
- cause and nature of injury;
- name, address and occupation of person giving the notice, if other than the injured person.

All Accident Books must be kept for a period of three years from the date of the last entry. An approved Accident Book (BI510) may be obtained from HMSO.

Hazardous substances

All hazardous substances must be strictly controlled and employers are required to ensure that employees do not have access to these. New Control of Substances and Hazardous Health Regulations (COSHH) were issued in 2002 to implement the European Union Chemical Agents Directive. These are relevant for all workplaces and cover hazardous substances such as airborne dusts, biological agents, chemicals, micro-organisms and respiratory sensitizers and are much more detailed than previously.

Workplace stress has become a major cause of absence in recent years. EU legislation is increasing the employers' duty of care in terms of mental health as well as physical health. An example of an Accident, Occupational Ill Health and Dangerous Occurrences Investigation and Reporting Procedure is shown in Figure 10.2.

**ACCIDENT, OCCUPATIONAL ILL HEALTH AND DANGEROUS
OCCURRENCES INVESTIGATION AND REPORTING PROCEDURE**

The following procedure should be used in cases of accidents that cause injury or ill health. This procedure covers events that result in individuals being hurt, dangerous occurrences as defined in The Reporting of Injuries, Diseases and Dangerous Occurrences Regulations 1995, cases of occupational ill health and in those instances where there have been incidents that have not resulted in personal injury but where property may have been damaged.

This procedure should be used whether the occurrence takes place on company premises or elsewhere where individuals are employed in work on behalf of the organization.

The procedure applies to all staff and also to temporary workers and also individuals who may be visiting the organization.

Departmental Heads are responsible for implementing this procedure within their area(s) of responsibility.

The Company's Health and Safety Officer is responsible for determining whether accidents have been adequately investigated and necessary actions taken and also whether adequate information has been recorded. The Company's Safety Officer, as defined in RIDDOR, will decide whether an accident needs to be reported to the HSE in accordance with the RIDDOR regulations and will be responsible for submitting all necessary reports.

General Guidance

1. ALL accidents must be recorded in the Accident Book.

2. Employees should report all accidents to their line manager. Accidents affecting contractors working on site or visitors to the company should report accidents or hazardous occurrences to the Departmental Head for whom they are working or visiting respectively.

3. The Safety Officer should be informed immediately if:
   ❑ an employee suffers a major injury, or is absent through injury for more than three days as a consequence of a work-related accident;

   ❑ a contractor or visitor is hospitalized following an accident on the company's premises.

Figure 10.2 A Sample Accident, Occupational Ill Health and Dangerous Occurrences Investigation and Reporting Procedure

---

ACCIDENT, OCCUPATIONAL ILL HEALTH AND DANGEROUS OCCURRENCES INVESTIGATION AND REPORTING PROCEDURE (continued)

4. The Safety Officer should be informed if an employee is diagnosed with a work-related or ill health condition defined within the RIDDOR regulations.

5. Accident reports should include enough detail of the accident and the circumstances leading up to it to assist in identifying the cause.

6. The accident should be reported promptly so that actions can be taken to prevent a recurrence. The accident report should be forwarded to the company's Safety Officer.

Reporting procedure for ALL accidents

Action must be taken immediately to prevent a recurrence or secondary accident. Where there is significant injury or dangerous occurrence, the scene of the accident must not be disturbed until it has been examined by the Safety Officer.

If the accident involves injury to a person, the following steps should be followed:

1. First aid and medical treatment as appropriate should be given to the injured employee.

2. Details of the accident should be recorded in the Accident Book and on the appropriate accident report form available from the Safety Officer.

3. The accident report form should be passed to the relevant Departmental Head and Safety Officer who will undertake the initial investigation to determine the underlying causes of the accident. Risk assessment should also be undertaken and revisions to controls/procedures instigated as quickly as feasible.

4. The Safety Officer or the Departmental Head should sign the report form to confirm the details.

5. The report is passed to the Safety Officer who will determine whether the accident has been appropriately investigated and actioned. Further investigations may take place at this stage.

6. Where appropriate the Safety Officer will pass the report to the HSE using documentation laid down in the RIDDOR regulations.

Figure 10.2 continued

**ACCIDENT, OCCUPATIONAL ILL HEALTH AND DANGEROUS
OCCURRENCES INVESTIGATION AND REPORTING PROCEDURE
(continued)**

7. Accidents that result in major injury, or injury requiring more than
    three days' absence from work, or where an employee has been
    taken to hospital, or where a dangerous occurrence has been
    identified plus certain occupational ill health conditions, will also be
    reported under the 'diseases' section of the RIDDOR regulations.

8. Copies of the report will be retained by the Safety Officer and
    by the Departmental Head.

Hazards

Reporting hazards should be treated as an internal safety communication
within departments. This mechanism will allow departments to ensure their
department conforms to health and safety arrangements. Hazards can be
reported to Departmental Heads using the appropriate form. Departmental
Heads can monitor their department's safety performance by analysing data
included in hazard reports.

Reporting of hazards relates to those areas that an individual is unable to
rectify themselves.

The employee who reports the hazard should take steps to minimize the
accident risk as far as is feasible without putting themselves at risk. This may
include communicating with those able to eliminate or reduce the risk, ie, the
Safety Officer.

The employee should complete a hazard report form and pass a copy to
the Departmental Head and Safety Officer.

The Departmental Head will investigate and take appropriate actions to
eliminate the hazard and control the accident risk. The Departmental Head may
seek advice from the Safety Officer as required.

A report should be produced by the Departmental Head and returned to
the person who reported the hazard. The Departmental Head should retain a
copy.

Figure 10.2 continued

OTHER RELEVANT LEGISLATION

There are six regulations that are crucial for anyone intending to set up a new business. These came about as a direct result of this country's membership of the European Union and have been incorporated into UK law:

- Management of Health and Safety at Work Regulations 1999 (Management Regulations);
- The Provision and Use of Work Equipment Regulations 1998;
- Workplace (Health, Safety and Welfare) Regulations 1992;
- The Health and Safety (Display Screen Equipment) Regulations 1992 (Display Screen Regulations);
- The Manual Handling Operations Regulations 1992 (Manual Handling Regulations);
- Personal Protective Equipment Work Regulations 1992 (PPE).

Other Regulations, which are also relevant for all organizations, are:

- Fire Precautions (Workplace) (Amendment) Regulations 1999;
- Employer's Liability (Compulsory Insurance) Regulations 1998;
- Working Time Directive and Working Time Regulations 1998;
- The Reporting of Injuries, Diseases and Dangerous Occurrences Regulations 1995;
- The Construction (Design and Management) Regulations 1994;
- Noise at Work Regulations 1989 (Noise Regulations);
- Electricity at Work Regulations 1989;
- Health and Safety (First Aid) Regulations 1981.

Scenario – The Fast Grow Seedling Company

You are the Manager with responsibility for Personnel and Health and Safety issues at The Fast Grow Seedling Company.

The supervisor who was working with a team of horticulturists who were planting out new seedlings has just informed you that Tom Brown, one of the team, has just fallen and grazed his arm on the edge of a spade.

Task

1. Identify the actions you need to take for the Fast Grow Seedling Company scenario.
2. What records will you need to make?

Scenario – Battles Brewery

You are the Human Resource Manager of Battles Brewery. Arthur Bell, your Brewery Manager, was investigating a leak on one of the large vats when he slipped on some spilled liquid and fell, injuring his back.

Task

Explain clearly the process you would follow to ensure that Battles Brewery conforms to current legislation.

Case study: Flavoursome Jellies Inc

You are the Personnel Manager at Flavoursome Jellies Inc. The Supervisor of the packing line has just informed you that Abby Turner, one of the packing room operatives, was stacking multiple shrink wrapped boxes of jellies onto a pallet at the end of the line when the load became unstable and toppled over onto her left leg and foot.

The Supervisor had immediately called for a first aider to take a look at Abby's injuries before contacting you.

Task

1. How will you investigate what has occurred at Flavoursome Jellies Inc?
2. Are there any other actions that you should take?

Useful contacts

Acas
Head Office
Brandon House
180 Borough High Street
London SE1 1LW
Telephone Helpline: 08457 474747

British Psychological Society
St Andrews House
48 Princess Road East
Leicester LE1 7DR
Tel: 0116 254 9568
E-mail: enquiry@bps.org.uk
Website: www.bps.org.uk

British Safety Council
70 Chancellors Road
London W6 9RS
Tel: 020 8741 1231
Website: www.britishsafetycouncil.co.uk

Chartered Institute of Personnel Development
CIPD House
Camp Road
Wimbledon
London SW19 4UX
Tel: 020 8971 9000
Website: www.cipd.co.uk

Commission for Racial Equality
CRE
St Dunstan's House
201–211 Borough High Street
London SE1 1GZ
Tel: 020 7939 0000
E-mail: info@cre.gov.uk
Website: www.cre.gov.uk

Confederation of British Industry
Centre Point
103 New Oxford Street
London WC1A 1DU
Website: www.cbi.org.uk

Department of Trade and Industry
DTI Enquiry Unit
1 Victoria Street
London SW1H 0ET
Tel: 020 7215 5000
Website: www.dti.gov.uk

Health & Safety Executive
Rose Court
2 Southwark Bridge
London SE1 9HS
Website: www.hse.gov.uk

Websites

The British Council of Disabled People
www.bcodp.org.uk

Royal Society for the Prevention of Accidents
www.rospa.co.uk/

Bibliography

Beattie, G (2003) *Visible Thought: The New Psychology of Body Language,* Routledge

Bratton, J and Gold, J (2003) *Human Resource Management: Theory and Practice,* Palgrave Macmillan

Briner, W, Hastings, C and Geddes, M (1996) *Project Leadership,* 2nd edn, Gower

Brown, A, (1995) *Organisational Culture,* Pitman Publishing

Cameron, A and Pearce, S (1995) *The Management Studies Handbook,* Pitman Publishing

Cardwell, M, (1996) *The Complete A–Z Psychology Handbook,* Hodder & Stoughton

Cole, G (2002) *Personnel and Human Resource Management,* Thomson Learning

Duncan, M et al (2004) *Health and Safety at Work Essentials,* 3rd edn, Law Pack Publishing

Edenbrough, R (1999) *Using Psychometrics: A Practical Guide to Testing and Assessment,* 2nd edn, Kogan Page

Essentials of Health & Safety at Work (1994) Health & Safety Executive

First Aid At Work: Your Questions and Answers Pack (1997) HSE

Fontana, D (1989) *Managing Stress*, The British Psychological Society and Routledge Ltd

Forsyth, P (2002) *Appraising Job Performance: How to Improve Job Satisfaction and Organisational Success* (Business Essentials), How to Books

Greenberg, J (1996) *Managing Behaviour in Organisations*, Prentice Hall

Guffey, M (2002) *Business Communication: Process and Product*, 4th edn, South-Western Publishing

Hayday, S and Bevan, S (2001) *Costing Sickness Absence in the UK: A Study Commissioned by Unum Ltd* (IES Report), Institute for Employment Studies

Jessop, G and H (1975) *Selection & Assessment at Work, Essential Psychology*, Methuen, London

Kettley, P and Kerrin, M (2003) *E-Recruitment – Is it delivering?* (IES Report), Institute for Employment Studies

Keuning, D (1998) *Management: A Contemporary Approach*, Pitman Publishing

Kline, P (1992) *Psychometric Testing in Personal Selection and Appraisal* (Croner's Human Resources), Croner Publications

Kline, P (2000) *The Handbook of Pyschological Testing*, 2nd edn, Routledge, London

Kossen, S (1994) *The Human Side of Organisations*, 6th edn, Harper Collins

Lawrie, Stephen M et al (2000) *Critical Appraisal for Psychiatrists*, Churchill Livingstone

Lynch, R (1997) *Corporate Strategy*, Pitman Publishing

Managing Absence: In Sickness and In Health, (1997) CBI

Munro Fraser, J (1966) *Employment Interviewing*, Macdonald and Evans

Purcell, J and Boxall, P (2002) *Strategy and Human Resources (Management, Work and Organisations)*, Palgrave Macmillan

Rodger, A (1973) _The Seven-Point Plan_, NIIP (Paper No. 5)

Stanton, N (2003) _Mastering Communication_, Palgrave Masters

Stranks, Jeremy (2001) _A Manager's Guide to Health and Safety at Work_, 6th edn, Kogan Page

Torrington, D (2001) _Human Resource Management_, F T Prentice Hall

Wainwright, GR (2003) _Body Language, Teach Yourself_, Hodder Arnold

Index

Further reading from Kogan Page

The Employer's Handbook: An Essential Guide to Employment Law, Personnel Policies and Procedures, 3rd edn, Barry Cushway, 2005

Handbook of Model Job Descriptions, Barry Cushway, 2003

Improving Employee Performance Through Workplace Coaching: A Practical Guide to Performance Management, Earl Carter and Frank McMahon, 2005

Manager's Guide to Health and Safety at Work, 7th edn, Jeremy Stranks, 2003

Mentoring in Action: A Practical Guide for Managers, 2nd edn, David Clutterbuck and David Megginson, 2005

Strategic Human Resource Management: A Guide to Action, 2nd edn, Michael Armstrong, 2000

The above titles are available from all good bookshops or direct from the publishers. To obtain more information please contact the publisher at the address below:

Kogan Page
120 Pentonville Road
London N1 9JN
Tel: 020 7278 0433
Fax: 020 7837 6348
www.kogan-page.co.uk